P9-BYM-992

SHAKEN
NOT
SHATTERED

SHAKEN
NOT
SHATTERED

MATTHEW HAGEE

Charisma
HOUSE
A STRANG COMPANY

Most Strang Communications Book Group products are available at special quantity discounts for bulk purchase for sales promotions, premiums, fund-raising, and educational needs. For details, write Strang Communications Book Group, 600 Rinehart Road, Lake Mary, Florida 32746, or telephone (407) 333-0600.

Shaken, Not Shattered by Matthew Hagee
Published by Charisma House
A Strang Company
600 Rinehart Road
Lake Mary, Florida 32746
www.strangbookgroup.com

This book or parts thereof may not be reproduced in any form, stored in a retrieval system, or transmitted in any form by any means—electronic, mechanical, photocopy, recording, or otherwise—without prior written permission of the publisher, except as provided by United States of America copyright law.

Unless otherwise noted, all Scripture quotations are from the New King James Version of the Bible. Copyright © 1979, 1980, 1982 by Thomas Nelson, Inc., publishers. Used by permission.

Scripture quotations marked KJV are from the King James Version of the Bible.

Design Director: Bill Johnson
Cover design by Bill Johnson

Copyright © 2009 by Matthew Hagee
All rights reserved

Library of Congress Cataloging-in-Publication Data:

An application to register this book for cataloging has been submitted to the Library of Congress.
International Standard Book Number: 978-1-59979-464-8

First Edition

09 10 11 12 13 — 9 8 7 6 5 4 3 2 1
Printed in the United States of America

To my father, my mentor, my hero, and my pastor: Thank you from the bottom of my heart for all you have done for me. You are more than an example to millions; you are the man of God I aspire to be.

To my wife and children: words will never express the love I have for each of you.

To my church: our best is yet to be!

CONTENTS

vii

Foreword

Leadership comes from mentorship. The secret to Joshua's success was that he had a Moses in his life. The secret to Elisha's success was that he had an Elijah in his life. The secret to young Timothy's success was that he had an apostle Paul in his life.

Matthew Hagee will be the first to tell you that he's a "chip off the old block." For decades Pastor John Hagee has written best-selling books and blessed millions with his powerful preaching. But now the moment has come for Matthew to step out of the shadows and share the wonderful insights God has given him.

Shaken, Not Shattered is an amazing book that will challenge you to believe that with God on your side, there are no boundaries—just possibilities—for your life. This book will teach you to expect the best to come out of the worst instead of the worst to come out of the best. God develops power in our lives through the pressures of the hard places. It's in those times that our faith may be shaken, but it will not be shattered.

Successful people usually fail more than others, but they don't quit. The player at a football game who gets knocked down the most is usually the one carrying the ball the most, but he also makes the most yards!

After years of close friendship with Matthew, I have noticed three qualities he possesses:

1. Transparent honesty

2. Authentic humility

3. Absolute integrity

Success or failure can be boiled down to one word—*character.* Matthew has great character. A man's character is not determined by his talent or his wealth but by what it takes to discourage him. I've observed Matthew in times of discouragement and trials; he has lived the words of this book and has earned the right to say them.

As you read through the pages of this book, God is going to develop in you an unshakable faith and character that will cause you to triumph over every challenge in order to win in life.

—JENTEZEN FRANKLIN
SENIOR PASTOR, FREE CHAPEL
NEW YORK TIMES BEST-SELLING AUTHOR, *FASTING*

Introduction

THE WORLD HAS been in this situation before—even if we have not. Everywhere you turn—the evening news, the morning newspaper, or a casual conversation with a close friend—you seem to get the message that things have never quite been as bad as they are right now. The more we attempt to analyze and solve the issues of our day, the more the equations seem to add up to hopelessness.

But before we go one step further, I want you to take hope in this fact: the world has been here before, even if we have not.

The world has faced tough times economically, politically, physically, and emotionally in various ways in each generation. There were times that seemed to shake the very core of the human spirit, and yet, in spite of the difficulty, we weren't shattered. Why? How? What steps did our predecessors take that we need to remember and employ? What secret ingredient did they use in the recipe for success and survival that we so desperately need right now?

First of all, our patriarchs and forefathers never forgot where they came from. They knew that they were created beings and that they were not all powerful in and of themselves. They were willing to accept the notion that their very existence required dependency on a source greater than self—a source that was stable and secure enough to see them through the most trying of times and give them the hope they needed to face tomorrow.

When the opportunity to write this book began, I would never have imagined that I would have a year that would demonstrate to me in so many ways what it is like to be shaken but not shattered. As my first deadline for this work approached, my family was informed that my father would require a quadruple bypass open-heart surgery in order to avoid a massive heart attack. Needless to say, that kind of news has a way of shaking you.

God was faithful over the next six weeks, and my dad made a complete and miraculous recovery. On the day he was released from the hospital to begin his rehab at home, my wife, Kendal, and I heard from the same cardiologist that her mother, my mother-in-law, would require an immediate heart-valve-replacement surgery in order to survive. As much as we appreciate medical professionals—doctors and nurses—for being there in moments of medical emergencies, we really would have preferred not to get to know them on a first-name basis.

Then, the Tuesday before Thanksgiving, my family received a phone call that my mother had been diagnosed with breast cancer and would undergo radically invasive surgery to ensure the disease would be cut out of her body. No sooner had we left the ICU and surgery wards for my father and mother-in-law than we found ourselves holding vigil there yet again. Through it all, God was faithful. I can gladly report to you that at this moment, every member of my family is alive and well and looking forward to the future.

In the last twelve months, I have not only observed the shaking of a nation's economy; the global political system; and the personal, emotional, and financial crises of many wonderful people, *but I have also been there myself.* And I can, with great confidence, share what I have learned through it all with you today. "He who is in you is greater than he who is in the world" (1 John 4:4).

No matter who you are, and regardless of what you are going through, you were created in the image of the almighty and unshakable God. The world around you may be trembling, but you have nothing to fear. You were created in the image of a magnificent God, and while your life may go through seasons of shaking, nothing in your life needs to shatter.

The first chapter of Hebrews quickly points out a very important truth: God made the world through His only begotten Son,

Jesus Christ. Listen to the description that is given of Christ in Scripture: "...who being the brightness of His glory and the express image of His person, and upholding all things by the word of His power..." (Heb. 1:3). Compare this description with the account of our own creation in Genesis: "Let Us make man in Our image" (Gen. 1:26). We were created in the express image of God, with the brightness of His glory and power. That's no small thing.

> No matter who you are, and regardless of what you are going through, you were created in the image of the almighty and unshakable God.

In the pages that follow, you will see what happens when you get back in touch with who God designed you to be—the genuine you, not what the world has tried to make you out to be or difficult times have dictated you have to be. You will discover how reconnecting with God will put you back in touch with your family, your faith, your physical health, your hope for the future, and the person who you are destined to be.

There is no limit to the life that is lived firmly planted in the power of the Creator of heaven and earth. It indeed enables you to be shaken and not shattered when the world is trembling.

Believe it, you are a real find, a joy in someone's heart. You're a jewel, unique and priceless. I don't care how you feel. Believe it, God don't make no junk.[1]

HERBERT BARKS

1

RECONNECTING WITH YOUR ORIGINAL DESIGN

"Don't Worry; We're Not Christians"

Fewer than eighteen months of age separate my sister Christina and me. Due to this "closeness," we have always had a tight relationship through every stage of life. When Tina, as I've always called her, went to kindergarten, I was upset that I couldn't go too. On my first day a year later, she walked me down the hall to my class, introduced me to my teacher, and informed everyone she would be across the hall if I needed her. And so it seemed to go until the day we graduated from college together, walking the stage on the same day, receiving our degrees within seconds of each other while my father delivered the commencement address.

I recall a day when we were in nursery school. Cornerstone Church was very young then, and on this particular day, each and every life associated with the church was suddenly shaken. My parents received a phone call late one evening. The caller informed them that the Medina family was on their way home when their vehicle was struck head-on by a speeding drunk driver. All the passengers in the car had been rushed to the hospital in an attempt to save their lives.

My mom and dad rushed to the hospital to see what could be done for Richard, Helen, and Meredith (the oldest of the Medina's children, who was the same age as Christina and me). Upon their arrival to the emergency room, the trauma surgeon spoke with them. His bloodstained garments and his fallen expression told the story. A few days later, our young church held three of the hardest funerals that my father's fifty-year ministry has ever known.

Tina and I didn't attend. At the ages of four and

three, we were simply too young to grasp what had happened to our nursery-school playmate and why we would not be able to see her again. The Sunday following the funerals, while on the way home from church, Christina began to interrogate our father about where her friend Meredith Medina was and when she would be coming back.

"Daddy, where's Meredith?"

Out of all the lectures he had heard in seminary and all the courses he had taken on his way to earning three degrees, none dealt with how you tell a child about death. "Well, honey, she's in heaven with Jesus," he said.

"Daddy, when is she coming back?"

"Baby, she's not coming back."

It was this announcement that brought tears to the corners of Tina's eyes. "But, Daddy, why not? I want to play with her."

My father has always quickly gotten to the bottom line. "Honey, Meredith had an accident and died, but she is with Jesus now, and because we are Christians and believe in Jesus, we will see her and her parents again when we go to be with Jesus."

No matter how sweetly he tried to say it, the message still didn't satisfy my sister. Her four-year-old mind suddenly ceased to worry about Meredith and began to swim with the notion that she might someday go where Meredith was because she was a Christian. At that moment, the conversation picked up in intensity: "But, Daddy, I don't want to go to heaven with Jesus! I want to stay here with you and Mommy!" Sunday brings a lot of challenges to a pastor, but this one was certainly unforeseen and nearly impossible to resolve.

It was at this time that I decided, even though I was only three years old, that I could be of some assistance to Dad. It was obvious to me that my sister wanted some assurance regarding her mortality—and that her fears had been brought on by the news that because we were Christians, we might not always live here on Earth. So I decided the best thing to do was tell her, "Don't worry, Tina. We are not Christians like Daddy. We are Mexicans like Mommy, and Mexicans never die!"

Tina's tears instantly dried, and the pouty bottom lip disappeared. In a totally satisfied and peaceful tone, she put her arm around my neck and said, "Thank you," as we rode the rest of the way home happy to know we were eternally secure.

The point is that even though the information I gave my sister was totally inaccurate, because I told her—with confidence—exactly what she wanted to hear, she was completely satisfied.

The same can be said of those who are searching for answers for their lives today. It really doesn't matter what the truth is as long as you can tell me what I want to hear, when I want to hear it, and in a way that is pleasant to hear. Then everything will be OK! The problem is that with the willingness to accept whatever answer you are looking for *rather than the truth*, you only postpone the reality that you are ignoring. How much better it would be to honestly confront the issue and make the change!

CONFRONTING THE REAL YOU

Who are you? Not the nine-to-five you or the weekend recreational extreme sports you or the summa cum laude class of '96 you—but the real you. Too many people find their identity in the wrong place, and I believe there is a good reason why.

We live in a culture that thrives on controversy. We live for prolonged public debates on everything under the sun. If you don't think so, just stand firmly on one side of an issue and you will meet someone who is equally passionate on the other side.

Controversy drives the ratings on the evening news, sells books and movie tickets, keeps talk radio alive, and makes you take a peek at the salacious titles on the magazines when you check out at the grocery store. There isn't an area of our lives not immersed in controversy.

> The Creation controversy removes our
> identity as beings handcrafted by God,
> fearfully and wonderfully made in His
> glorious image.

There is political controversy, economic controversy, social controversy, religious controversy, educational controversy, great big giant controversy, and little itty-bitty small controversy. However, the controversy that has cost us the most is the one that has stolen the identity of an entire generation: the *Creation controversy.*

Do you want to know why we are shaking as a society? The simple answer is that we have forgotten who we are and what we were designed to be. We have lost touch with all that kept us grounded. We no longer have a sense of certainty about who we are and why we are here. We have made a controversial debate of the origin of the world and how life began in the genesis of time. At the expense of our self-confidence, we have made an argument of the truth rather than accepting it.

On the issue of Creation, the debate has raged from the classroom to the courtroom, from the pulpit to the Oval Office, and back again. We have heard so much on the topic that many have taken the position of "Who really cares?" and "What difference does it make?"

Here's the difference and danger of this debate and why we should really care. What hang in the balance of this controversy are not conservative or liberal views on minor issues such as economic subsidies and tax-supported programs; the lines that are being drawn here are not between red states or blue states, believer or nonbeliever. Where you stand on this issue determines who you are and how you see yourself.

The Creation controversy has cost us a great deal, whether you recognize it or not. We have reduced the most magnificent six days the world has ever known down to an argument. The impact is undeniably clear—it has changed the world's perspective of the Greatness that created us and of the Unshakable Rock from which we were fashioned. The generation that forgets where it has come from will not know where to look when it gets lost.

When you read the Creation account, you'll discover that from the very first chapter of the Bible, it was centered on you. The sun is not just a burning ball of gas suspended in space; it was hung so you could have light in the day. The moon is more than a place for the shuttle to land; God designed it for you to see and know each night how much He cares for you. As a matter of fact, the writer of the eighth psalm notices all of the wonders in the sky and relates to them this way: "What is man that You are mindful of him?" (Ps. 8:4). It's as if to say, "Lord, what made You think so much of me that You would go to such a great length to do all of this?"

Not only were the heavens created for you, but also land was given to you to walk upon and live on, and water was supplied as a precious resource for every life. If you reduce the sun to the scientific explanation of a cosmic fireball and the earth to a by-product of a *big bang*, then when you wake up in the morning, you have no reason or motivation for saying *thank you* for the daylight, and you forget to give the Almighty the appreciation

He so richly deserves for all that He provided for you in the span of just one week.

The heavens and the earth are not the only things that seem to get devalued by this controversy—you and I suffer also. The Creation controversy removes our identity as beings handcrafted by God, fearfully and wonderfully made in His glorious image. We have now become like all the rest of the *stuff* taking up space on this planet—just here today by chance and maybe gone tomorrow.

HOW DID YOU GET HERE?

Creation is more than a controversy; it is the foundation of your life. You were created out of something. When you read the Creation account in Genesis, you will notice this pattern: Everything that God created, from the elements in the heavens down to the last detail on Earth, was *called out of something.* He called light out of darkness; He called land out of water; He called fish out of the ocean, animals out of the dust of the ground, and plants out of the earth. All of these things have a relationship dependent upon their source. You cannot escape this truth: everything has a source; nothing by itself is independent.

For example, a fish is dependent on water to survive. Plants must remain in contact with the ground in order to grow. An animal designed to live and breathe on land will drown if you force it to exist under water, where it was not created to go. Why? Because the earth and water are the foundational sources for animals, plants, and fish.

———————

The generation that forgets where it has
come from will not know where to look
when it gets lost.

———————

Your source is none other than God. You were created to remain in contact with Him. Before God was finished in Genesis, He created something unlike anything anywhere else, something superior to the animals and lower than the angels, a being with the ability to design, build, create, subdue, and have dominion. You were God's masterpiece, and He didn't want to use just any material to create you. When He created you, He chose the absolute best. For you, the sky and land and sea simply would not do as a source. So when God chose your source, *He spoke to Himself* and said, "Let Us make man in Our image" (Gen. 1:26), and man became a living being.

You did not just happen. You were created from the substance of the Almighty, and because of this fact, you, like all other created things, cannot properly survive or function apart from your foundational source.

If you remove a fish from water or a plant from the ground, it will lose its identity. They cease to exist in the way they were created. The fish may become your dinner and the plant your side salad, but they are no longer growing or producing.

The same is true with you and me. Remove us from our source, which is almighty God, and we cease to grow and produce. Oh sure, we may become something else, but we have lost our true identity.

The solution is to ignore the controversy and reconnect with your source. Stop seeing yourself as the world sees you, and start seeing what God sees—His glory on display. Refuse to let the debate and banter of lesser beings distract you from the truth; you are the handmade masterpiece of God Almighty.

You did not just happen. You were created from the substance of the Almighty, and because of this fact, you, like all other created things, cannot properly survive or function apart from your foundational source.

What is in God can be found in you, but only when you are in proper connection with your source. Because He is great, you can be great. Because He is love, you will love others and yourself. Because He is all powerful, you can live without limit. Because He is unshakable, you can endure the most trying times and remain unshattered.

Remembering your source is the first major step to surviving difficult times, because doing so answers the question of who you are and tells you all that you can be. You are not what is written on your résumé; you are not what your degrees and plaques on the wall proclaim. You are a child of God, created for His glory and born to be something great!

Four steps to achievement: Plan purposefully. Prepare prayerfully. Proceed positively. Pursue persistently.[1]

WILLIAM A. WARD

2

Priorities Will Get You Where You Want to Go

You Will Possess What You Pursue

History records a man whose first major failure came in business in 1831. He quickly pursued an office in the state legislature and was defeated in 1832. He attempted yet another business in 1833 without any success. In 1834, he met a young lady and fell in love with her, but she died in 1835 before they could be married. He suffered an emotional breakdown in 1836. He was defeated for a congressional seat in 1843 and again in 1848. He then attempted running for the Senate in 1855 and lost. The next year he ran for the office of vice president of the United States and lost again. In 1859, he ran for the Senate once again and was once again defeated. Finally, in 1860, the man who signed his name "A. Lincoln" was elected as the sixteenth president of the United States.[2] He pursued his purpose until he possessed it.

History states that the reason he had such a fire in his soul to continue on even though he experienced one setback after another came from a business trip he made to the city of New Orleans. Young Lincoln stood on the docks of the New Orleans harbor and watched as a ship was offloading slaves who were then sold at auction, right there as they came off the ship. He saw children pulled from mothers' arms and separated by a bid and bill of sale like merchandise and property with no thought of their humanity. As he watched this sight, with tears in his eyes Lincoln vowed to do whatever was required of him to see the evil of slavery in America come to an end.

Therefore, with his mind firmly made up and his priorities established, he pursued one office of influence and public service after another to do what he could to make a change. He accomplished his goal at a great price and showed all who would follow that you can and will possess what you are willing to pursue. One of the many lessons learned by those who have studied the life of Abraham Lincoln is the power of priorities.

The pages of history, and of the Bible, are filled with illustrations that teach us this principle. Some of these inspire us to press on, and others remind us to be careful of what we wish for because we just might get it! But without a doubt, the priorities of each generation have determined not only their quality of life but also the quality of life for those who follow. In times of uncertainty, when the things that you thought were solid and secure begin to crumble, you will forfeit all that you do not value, and what you cling to will inform the world of your true priorities in life.

All too tragically, there are those who have demonstrated that their true priorities are not as selfless as those of President Lincoln. *Faith, family,* and *country* do not describe the pursuit of many today. When the world begins to shake economically, many throw their families to the wind in pursuit of the *almighty dollar.* When the nation faces dark hours and needs leaders who are willing to have the courage to take responsibility for their actions, it seems political finger-pointing and the "blame game" develop further into art forms instead of leaders demonstrating accountability and the courage to truly make a change.

The problem is that our misguided priorities have cost us a high premium for the "quality" of life we now possess. Because of our pursuit of self-ishness, we now possess a divorce rate where 41 percent of first marriages, 60 percent of second marriages, and 73 percent of third marriages are dissolved by the courts.[3] Because of our pursuit of greed, we now possess a global economic crisis. We have educated our children that responsibility and work are not nearly as powerful as entitle-ment, and, in doing so, we are reaping what we have sown: a generation riddled with ingratitude and disrespect.

It is time to reconnect with our source! By reconnecting with your source and living your life as it was originally designed to be lived, you enable yourself to set priorities that will get you where you want to go and, more importantly, where God called you to be.

ARE THE GOOD OLD DAYS GONE?

I have had conversations with some very precious people, such as my grandmother and other elderly figures whom I love, and I have heard them referencing "the good old days." For example, my grandmother has told me there was a day in America when "even the unchurched nonbeliever had good morals." She would put it this way: "Son, it used to be that even the bad were still good."

Nowadays it seems unethical behavior and immorality are rampant in nearly every area of life, and when you look at our society, you see a sliding scale of corruption instead of a clear line drawn between right and wrong. People have lost confidence in many established authorities—whether they are political, religious, or educational. We wonder if there is any good left in the world anymore, and we find ourselves thinking, "Are the good old days gone?"

What happened? What caused our society to slip so far so fast? I can tell you the reason; it is because we now possess what we pursued: a society without God.

Back at the point in America when even *the bad* were *still good*, a very simple yet profound source was still acknowledged: Every child in America went to a school where the Ten Commandments hung on the wall. Whether they recognized it or not, the truth locked in those ten lines greatly impacted their lives.

The Bible tells us, "My word...shall not return to Me void" (Isa. 55:11). Every time a child saw the Ten Commandments on the schoolhouse wall, the concepts of honesty, integrity, honor, kindness, and trust entered into that child's subconscious. This had a profound impact. At the foundation of our educational system was the source of responsibility and strength: God Himself.

Unfortunately, camouflaged under the title of "civil liberty," an

23

organization sued the school system for influencing its students with such disruptive thoughts as "Thou shall not kill," "Honor your father and mother," "Thou shall not lie or steal," and "Thou shall have no other gods before Me." They used words like *freedom* and *rights* to launch an all-out attack on God Himself, and in doing so disconnected our system of education from the source of all knowledge.

When we removed the Ten Commandments and prayer from school, we declared that it was our desire as a nation to pursue an education apart from God. Now, two generations later, we have tragically possessed what we pursued. Our leaders legislate as if God didn't exist, because they were educated in a system that taught them to live this way. When you govern in such a fashion, you not only corrupt the nation, but you also condemn the next generation.

We have taught our children in science class that life does not begin in the womb and that what grows during the nine months of gestation is not a human being but a harvestable blob of flesh that can and should be used for the purpose of science and medical research. This is the reason why our leaders have no problem passing laws enabling state-funded abortions. When they were educated as children, they were not taught that man was a divinely created being; they were taught that he was just another animal.

We have removed "Thou shall not kill" from the wall, and the bullet-riddled bodies of students now line the halls.

We have removed the concept "Thou shall not commit adultery," and now the faculty is sexually involved with the student body.

We have educated an entire generation—from kindergarten to college—without the concept of God even being allowed in one chapter of one book, and we wonder why we are shaking as a society. For better or for worse, it is true that you will possess what you pursue.

WHERE DO WE BEGIN?

So, how do we correct it? What can we do to reverse what has been done and to see if there is an opportunity to revive *the good old days* once again? The first thing we must do is establish priorities that will keep us in pursuit of our source. If what you wish for is a life filled with peace, joy, and success, then pursuing the source of peace, joy, and success should certainly be your top priority.

However, there are usually some things that need to change in our lives before this can become a reality. We must recognize that God is not here to fit into our busy lives and exist only when and where it is convenient for us. Remember the first commandment? "Thou shall have no other gods before Me." That means that in order for the King of kings to rule in our lives, our personal desires have to be dethroned.

I know a lot of people who feel life would be so much easier if God could function on their schedules and fulfill their purposes, but the exact opposite is true. You and I are here to function on His schedule for His glory and to pursue His purpose. Without a doubt, every unshakable life has at least one thing in common: this type of person puts God first on his or her list of priorities; for this there is no substitute.

When God is first in your life, rather than just a part of your life, you can quit trying to squeeze His unlimited blessings into your limited existence. The moment you make Him your top priority, you gain access to His abundance in every area of your life because He is now the one in control.

Be Willing to Lose Control

Have you noticed how tenaciously we thirst for control? Mankind loves control. We look at the world through the lens of domination. We want to control everything—even nature. If a mountain is in the way, tunnel through it. If there is a river to cross, dam it up and build a bridge over it.

We even try to control our relationships. It's called *manipulation*, and it takes on multiple forms. There is financial manipulation, emotional manipulation, and physical manipulation, and all of them boil down to one word: *control*. No matter what the problem may be, according to man's way of thinking, as long as we can manipulate it, we can solve it because we then control it.

If God is going to be the first priority in your life then you are going to have to relinquish control. Don't get me wrong; control is not a bad thing when you view it in the proper perspective, but you need to recognize where your control ends and God's control begins.

Everything that you have ever had control over has been given to you by God for you to manage, not own. Note the difference!

We like to view ourselves in the *ownership role*. From our earliest days, we claim everything we put our hands on as our own.

My two-year-old son is starting to talk. I can make out some words, but others require the gift of interpretation, but the one word that is loud and clear and can be heard a mile away is *mine*. Why? Because he, like the rest of us, wants to be in control. At this point in his life, you could say he is somewhat possessed by his possessions. He knows which blanket in the house belongs to him and will do whatever he has to do to defend it from all invaders, foreign and domestic.

If his sister tries to defile his quilt by laying it over one of her baby dolls that she is putting to sleep, the declaration of war is made and can be heard echoing down the halls of our quiet domicile as my little boy shouts, "MINE!" He'll lose his joy, abandon whatever toy he was freely playing with at the moment, and exert whatever force is needed to reclaim what he perceives belongs to him.

The truth is, the blanket of which he is so possessive isn't his at all; it's really mine. I bought it, and I gave it to him. It is indeed his to enjoy for a time, but ownership belongs to me. Many of us approach life the same way. It's our job, our house, our car, our family, our church, our city, our nation—and we take total ownership because we want total control. This reality assigns ownership to the wrong person. We are not the owners; our Father is. What we have, He has given us to enjoy.

In truth, the more we try to take over our lives, the more totally out of control we become on every level. The only way to regain what has been lost is to play the role God designed us to play and stop trying to be the ruler of the universe and all surrounding galaxies. Get out of God's way, and put Him back where He belongs—in control. Understand that we have nothing unless God, who is the owner of all things and is in total control, allows us to have it.

He may allow us to manage some things for a time, but it all belongs to Him. Your job—where you work during the week—is the one He gave you so that you'd have the resources to buy what you need. Therefore, when you go to work, don't go intending only to please the boss in the corner office. Go to work every day ready to show the Lord you appreciate the job He has allowed you to have.

Your family is the one He blessed you with. You have a very real role to play within the walls of your house, and in order for the blessings of God to be on your life, you must be willing to live out His purpose in the home. Remember, it's not your family—it's His.

Your church happens to be His house, the place where His Spirit dwells. For you to even attempt to get in His way within the structure of the sanctuary is to invite His judgment upon your life. Your nation is the one established by His grace. You cannot ignore your responsibility to the land where you dwell. To say that our national problems are not your personal problem is to ignore the facts and deny reality.

Let there be no doubt; God indeed has a role for you in every aspect of life. When you allow a proper set of priorities to establish the role you play, you will discover that your life will be filled with enormous influence and power. However, no matter how much power and influence you possess, you will always serve in the capacity of *management* and not in *ownership*.

You may be allowed to manage certain things for a lifetime and others only for a few moments, but no matter what, you cannot lose sight of the fact that the source of it all is God. The point: *God is in control.* He is to be your first priority because He is the owner, and we are the servants.

CAN GOD TRUST YOU WITH HIS STUFF?

When God is first in your life and your greatest desire is to do His will, then every resource you have is available to Him because you understand it all belongs to Him anyway. The moment God sees you as a person who can be trusted with possessions, you suddenly qualify to receive more than you had before!

Do you know what made Abraham great? He trusted in God. Even to the point that when he didn't have a clue what God was doing, he still trusted Him. Abraham's ability to trust the Lord is what made it possible for him to go so far as to offer his son Isaac as a sacrifice when God requested it. Abraham understood that the child God had given to Sarah and him was actually not theirs at all.

Isaac came from God, and he belonged to the Lord. If the Lord required him to be sacrificed, then Abraham was simply responsible to manage the task that he was given. Not every chore you are asked to do in your role as a manager will be pleasant, but your willingness and obedience will determine how much God can trust you. In Genesis 22:12, the angel of the Lord told Abraham, "Now I know that you fear God, since you have not withheld your son, your only son, from Me."

Was Isaac precious to Abraham? Without a doubt! He was so loved that Abraham named him *the son of laughter*. However, although Isaac was terribly loved, Abraham knew he could trust God with what he loved the most. It was this kind of trust that enabled Abraham to be the recipient of blessings that others could only dream about. He was called *the friend of God* (James 2:23). He was blessed in his life to the point that you would have to number the stars in the sky and the sands of the earth to calculate all that he received. He was described as being very rich in livestock, silver, and gold. Abraham was increased in his life, and the lives of his descendants and heirs were increased because God could trust him.

No matter how much power and influence you possess, you will always serve in the capacity of management and not in *ownership*.

When your priorities are centered in your source, and God can trust you with His resources, your priorities will get you where you want to go.

WHERE DO OTHERS FIT?

The next priority in your life, after the Lord, should be other people—those in the world around you. For me, that list includes, in this order: my wife and children, my extended family, and my church. Once you've decided to reconnect with God, the next place to start reconnecting is at home.

The desire to *live for ourselves* is an epidemic in our society. It seems we have adopted this mind-set: if it is to our benefit and someone else's detriment, so be it. What is so horrifying about this mind-set is that it means *no relationship is safe.*

There has been a notable increase through the years of the disenchantment with marriage. Without a doubt, the root of divorce is selfishness. But consider these latest trends in our society: parents are harming and abusing their children, children are being arrested for atrocities committed against parents, and siblings are being indicted for murdering their brothers and sisters—all for the sole purpose of having what they want when they want it. From all appearances, it seems there is no limit to selfish men.

The evening news carries one story after another of a mother or a boyfriend or a relative who is being arrested for some monstrosity committed against a defenseless child. Why? Because other people no longer have a place of priority in our lives. We have truly lost touch with each other. We have devalued life to the point that it is considered expendable for the sake of convenience.

However, if you are ever going to be the person of influence that you were created to be, then others will need to take their proper place of priority in your life. You can begin by identifying ways that you can be a blessing to others. Place their needs in front of yours, and consider it a joy when those around you succeed. Answer these questions honestly: Where do others fit in your life? Are you there for them, or are they there for you? You will never truly know the power that relationship possesses until you decide to *be there* for the other person—no matter what.

This is true on all levels. As a society, the greatest moment in a nation's history comes when people put others first. It happens when you are willing to lay down your life for another and they are willing to lay down their life for you. Self-sacrifice is the down payment on the kind of relationships that have the power to overcome the most impossible of situations. Every great church is built by men and women of God who will sacrifice their lives for their brothers and sisters in Christ. If the next generation is to succeed, it will be the result of the self-sacrifice of the previous generation. If a marriage is going to make it, then self-sacrifice by a husband for his wife and a wife for her husband will be the source of the success.

If you want to set a priority that will get you where you want to go in your marriage, then start living for your spouse rather than asking him or her to live for you.

I have had this conversation with a lot of married couples, and, in most cases, each person's immediate reaction is, "I do put him [or her] first!" Then each person begins to list all of the things he or she does for the spouse. If it is the husband, he will describe how he gets up and goes to work so that he can provide for the family. If it is the wife, she will list all of the things that she does on a regular basis so *the king* will feel at home in his castle.

But the reality is this: their initial reactions do not demonstrate why their spouse is a priority; they are more of a justification for why each one feels unappreciated. The husband wants to know why she can't be more understanding when he wants to relax and watch the ball game; after all, he's been working hard for her all week long, right? The wife, on the other hand, wants to know why he can't be more willing to go to the mall on Saturday instead of watching the game of the week on TV; after all, she's kept the house all week and wants some time with him.

Prioritizing others in your life has to do with *placement*, not effort. For example, when a wife begins to badger her husband about the time he is spending away from home and his family because of work, what is really being communicated is, "What means more to you—me and the kids or the job?" She wants to know, "Where do we fit? What is our place in your life?"

> You will never truly know the power that relationship possesses until you decide to be there for the other person— no matter what.

I do not know a woman on the face of the earth who wants to hear her husband answer that question with this response: "Honey, you are right. I have been away at work and earning money so we can pay the bills and have nice things, but I feel terribly guilty about how much time I am not spending with you, so I quit! We are going to sell the house and the cars. We are going to move in with my mother and share her spare bedroom. You are never going to own another new garment or pair of shoes. We are never going to take another vacation. The kids are going to have to beg, borrow, and steal to get a college education, but, baby, at least we are going to be together."

Relationships that stand the test of time
require self-sacrifice.

That's not the answer she is looking for. If the issue had been *time*, that answer would be sufficient, but it's not about time. It's not about the hours of effort that you put in at the office instead of at home. It's about *placement*. When your wife tells you that you're spending too much time at work, what she is really saying is, "Work has become your priority, and I am starting to wonder where my place is with you." It's not about the *amount* of time you spend; it's about the *quality* of time you spend.

So, what's the solution? Make her your priority. When you go to work, do a little something every now and then to tell your wife that even though you are not by her side, she is the number one thing on your mind. Take some of the company letterhead and write her a love letter; believe me, it will be the best stamp you ever stuck in the mail. Send her an e-mail, a text message, or a bouquet of flowers that reminds her where she is placed in your life's priorities. Call her before you leave the office to tell her you'll be home soon, and ask her if there is anything that you can do for her on the way home. Remind her that even though you are not by her side, she is still on your mind and first and foremost in your heart.

You may be reading this and thinking, "Yeah, right. Do you know what the guys at the office would say if I did that?" My response is this: The last time I checked, you were trying to spend the rest of your life with your spouse, not with your colleagues. If loving your wife out loud washes off too much of your *Rambo* image, then you weren't all that tough to begin with.

Relationships that stand the test of time require self-sacrifice. This is especially true with your spouse. The greatest benefit for placing your spouse's needs over your own is that he or she will return the favor. When he or she is number one in your heart and mind, you become number one within theirs.

WHERE DO YOU FIT?

The last person on your list of priorities should be you. When you pursue God and reconnect with Him as your source, He will impact the relationships you have with those around you and empower them to fulfill His purpose for your life. When you discover who God is and what He wants your life to be, you will realize that the last person you need to reconnect with is yourself.

It is never too late to establish a set of priorities that will enable you to possess the best things in life—no matter how difficult the environment is that you live in. Did you know that there is a real difference between what you want and what you wish for? What you wish for is something you constantly talk about but never pursue. What you want is something that you pursue until you possess it.

A lot of people are willing to wish for the best things in life, but few are willing to pursue the best until they possess it. It is time to quit wishing for things to be different and to start making a difference. What do you want out of life? Is it the satisfaction and enjoyment of success or status quo by just keeping up with the Joneses? Are you willing to do what is required to have God's absolute best for your family, your finances, and yourself? The choice is yours. Your priorities will lead the way.

Goals are not only absolutely necessary to motivate us. They are essential to really keep us alive.[1]

ROBERT SCHULLER

3

Make a Decision, and Go for It!

Victory or Death

The United States of America was birthed by a group of men who were not afraid to make a decision. This fact has been well documented from the genesis of our nation. The oaths and commitments that our Founding Fathers made in order to see the land of liberty become a reality came with great risk and threat of loss, but they were willing to pay the price for what they believed was the will of the Almighty and the divine purpose for their lives.

One decision that may have indeed saved this nation in one of its most desperate hours came from General George Washington himself on the night of December 25, 1776. Under his command, the Continental army had suffered a series of defeats and retreated to the Pennsylvania shore of the ice-filled Delaware River. They camped there—exhausted, demoralized, and uncertain of their futures.

General Washington faced a dire set of circumstances. Support for the Revolution was dwindling, and the contracts between his enlisted soldiers and the army would soon expire. At this moment, he seemed to make a decision that defied all logic and reason and that stretched his very limited and depleted resources to the extreme.

Conventional European warfare chose to engage in battle in the spring, summer, and fall, while resting and encamping during the winter. The British had defeated the Continental army in every engagement that summer and felt that as soon as the snow thawed, the fighting would be over and the Revolution crushed. It was this very fact that caused Washington to take action.

On the night of December 25, he called all of his

officers into his tent to share with them the battle plan. Written in quotes at the top of the page of paper for all his officers to see were the words "Victory or death." Those three words informed every man in his command of Washington's resolve in this conflict. His message was very clear. This decisive action was going to have one of two results—there was no middle ground. In order to be successful, each and every solider had to be committed to going all the way.

The final plans were made, and the preparations set. The soldiers began the snowy march toward their fate—some not even wearing shoes. The Delaware would be no easy crossing, considering the swift current and the huge chunks of ice floating downstream. The nine-mile march to Trenton would be difficult for these men who were short on sleep and even shorter on food and strength. However, on Christmas night 1776, General Washington made a decision, and in spite of the risks, he went for it.

The surprise attack was more than a victory over the superior forces that they faced; it was a moral and emotional victory for those who thought defeating the British was impossible. It was an announcement to the world watching from across the Atlantic in Europe that the American army was indeed a force to be reckoned with. It was an announcement to all of the thirteen struggling

American colonies that no matter what they had suffered thus far, the dream of liberty was still alive. None of it would have occurred unless someone had been willing to make the decision.

Our lives are truly dictated by the decisions we choose to make or refuse to make. All too often fear is the driving force that determines our path. In this chapter, I want you to be able to make your decisions from a position of confidence and certainty. You were not created to live in fear; you were born to take action. If you are going to succeed in life, make the decision to be successful, and refuse all other options. Your choices may not always produce the result you desire, but if you resolve to continue rather than quit, then every decision you make will be a stepping-stone toward future successes. This much is certain: the surefire way to fail is to do nothing. So make a decision, and go for it.

Dictating Your Decisions

Your priorities will dictate the decisions that you make for yourself, your family, and your future. Up to this point, it has been my purpose to enable you to see yourself as the by-product of the creative genius of God on display and as a person who has a powerful and influential role to play in the lives of others in the world around you. Before you can make any truly meaningful decisions, these truths must be firmly established in your mind. To help you see how these elements are connected, allow me to break it down into smaller bites.

If you do not see yourself as divinely created by God, then your perspective is centered on the assumption that life is more chance than choice. It really doesn't matter what you choose to do; the chips are going to fall where they may. From your perspective, life will be just a series of events that happen, and you will see yourself as powerless to do anything about it.

This worldview will place individuals as the center of their own universe and cause all of their reasoning to begin and end solely with how their choices will affect them. Since the person with this worldview is always looking out for number one, and his confidence and faith are in his own strength and resources, everything he does will come from a position of selfish motivation. When the world around a self-centered individual begins to experience any kind of unexpected turmoil, he will cut and run and look for someone else to take the fall while he takes the bailout. Why is this true? Because self-centered people are not into sacrifice, and self-sacrifice is a requirement to survival when it comes to difficult times. When the driving force behind your decisions is simply you and you alone, it won't take long for your world to come unraveled.

If you intend to succeed in life regardless of the struggle, it means you have to make decisions that others are unwilling or too afraid to make. You have to go for it full-steam ahead. The choices you will make in life are without a doubt very difficult.

The sum total of your life will be composed of your choices. If your choices are driven by fear of others, their opinions, and their perspectives, you will always have your destiny determined by the mind-set of the masses. When your decisions are rooted in God, your source, and the motivation behind your choices is the betterment of others, then you can rest assured that the path you're on—no matter how difficult—will lead you to a place of great fulfillment in every way.

DON'T JUST TALK—TAKE ACTION

The most important decision you can make is this: are you going to be a person of action or a person of mere words? Words never solved a problem; they simply delayed the outcome. I think it's laughable when world leaders say, "We are going to get together for talks." If you really want to know why very few of the world's problems ever get resolved and most seem to continually get worse, it's because everybody likes to talk, and very few are willing to take action. The ability to address the problem is one thing; the willingness to get the job done is a totally different story. The people who survive in a world falling apart are people of action; these are the ones who get the job done.

The world we live in is in desperate need of people who will take action *and* be willing to sacrifice to get the job done. It is not just in the birth of our nation where we can see self-sacrifice paying the price for survival. Every chapter of our history is filled with people of action who were willing to make a sacrifice in the most difficult of times. Their deeds were the down payment on the quality of life for the next generation. Forgetting where we come from as a nation is just as devastating as forgetting where we come from spiritually. Both will cause you to betray yourself and destroy what others have paid such a high price to provide.

Compare the self-sacrificing America of yesterday with the America of today. We have become a society filled with a sense of entitlement and self-gratification. *Self-sacrifice* is not a word that is commonly heard in our society anymore. In removing this trait from our character, we have bankrupted the true quality of life, liberty, and the pursuit of happiness for those who follow. How has this happened in such a short period of time? It has happened because we have raised a generation that decided that compromise is greater than sacrifice.

COMPROMISE VS. SACRIFICE

The difference between compromise and sacrifice is pretty simple. *Compromise* makes everyone comfortable and is usually self-motivated. *Sacrifice* requires total commitment and is totally selfless. The world around you is not only overwhelmed with controversy; it is also saturated with compromise.

The sum total of your life will be composed of your choices.

In a compromise, mutual concessions are made by each party in order to sire up a give-and-take agreement that sees both getting what they wanted. They may act like it is a *major sacrifice*, but most of the time it is nothing more than theatrics and lip service. True sacrifice is demonstrated when you are willing to lay down your life *without* the promise of anything in return. The words written at the top of General Washington's battle plan described sacrifice: "Victory or death." He was willing to do whatever was required in order to see the purpose of liberty and the cause of freedom fulfilled.

That kind of *all-or-nothing* approach is nearly extinct in the world today. There was a time in America when people saw themselves as a small part of the big picture rather than as *the* picture. This view was reflected in their work ethic. Seeing the company succeed meant that they succeeded, and that was the goal of the greater good. Now it seems that every morning when you peruse the morning headlines, there is another executive who has pillaged a company for his own benefit and left a lot of people desperately stranded. The only way this behavior can possibly be explained is that selfish ambition and greed have seared their conscience to the point of not considering the consequences of their actions and decisions.

> Compromise makes everyone
> comfortable and is usually self-motivated.
> Sacrifice requires total commitment and
> is totally selfless.

In America's earlier days, you could find sacrifice everywhere —in businesses, neighborhoods, government, churches, and communities. However, the current trends have elevated compromise over sacrifice.

Apply this principle to marriage. Do you know why so many marriages end in divorce? Because marriage is a relationship that requires sacrifice rather than compromise in order to survive. If your marriage is going to endure the most difficult days and only grow stronger in the struggle, you have to lay your life down—not compromise.

Read these wedding vows, which are filled with sacrifice:

> Do you promise in covenant before God and these witnesses to be a wedded husband or wife—faithful in plenty and want, joy and sorrow, sickness and health, better or worse, forsaking all others, and giving yourself only to the other as long as you both shall live?

Not one ounce of compromise is involved. Marriage is not a relationship based on compromise; it is built on sacrifice.

The nature of compromise says, "What's in it for me?" Sacrifice says, "No matter what, for better or worse, I'll do what it takes because I'm in it for you."

Apply this to our nation. When we as a society cease to be a people of compromise and start taking action that is centered on self-sacrifice, then we will once again be the great society that Ronald Reagan, one of our most prominent leaders, described as a "shining city on a hill."

For this to take place, the government will need to stop talking and spending and start leading. When this happens, our schools will stop processing students and start educating individuals. Our churches will need to stop trying to make everyone comfortable and start telling the truth that sets men free. Our homes will need to stop being filled with disconnected individuals and start being filled with families. Our children will need to stop searching aimlessly for leadership and direction and be willing to emulate the fathers and mothers who laid down their lives in order for someone else to succeed.

All of the above are not by-products of compromise; they are the rewards to those who have made the decision to live a life of self-sacrifice.

THE POP QUIZ OF DESTINY

Know that decisions centered on the right basis don't always come without risks. All decisions have risks. I stated earlier that most people base their decisions in fear created by uncertainty. I want you to be confident in the choices you make, and in doing so, I won't deny the risk but will give you the ability to calculate them with assurance. When it comes to counting the cost and taking the risk, I invite you to utilize what I call *the pop quiz of destiny.*

If you are not good at quizzes, don't worry; this one is short and open book. There are two questions to this quiz. Question one requires you to look back at your past. Question two causes you to focus on your future.

Question one

The first question that you ask yourself when it comes to analyzing the risk involved in your decision is this one: "Has God brought me thus far to lose it all now?"

Quickly take a moment and flip through the pages of your past. Has God protected you, provided for you, empowered you, healed you, helped you, and allowed you to come this far just to quit? Can you now see why reconnecting with your source and knowing where you came from is so important? How can you answer this first question of destiny unless God is the foundation for the answer?

God's plan for your life is not to
leave you short of fulfilling your purpose,
so you have no reason to worry about
the risks involved in making the decision
that you face.

Every time I face an issue that seems to require a truly *make-it-or-break-it* decision, the first thing I do is look at all that God has brought me through. When I consider all He's already done for me, I rarely have to ask if this is all He has in store. When I see all He has already done, I certainly know He's not through with me yet.

God has looked out for me from the very beginning. When my mother was pregnant with me, she thought she had been exposed to a woman who had German measles while at church one Sunday. Knowing this posed a threat to her pregnancy, she called her doctor to see what he might recommend she do. He coldly responded, "Well, come into the office, and we can terminate the pregnancy since this child will be born with abnormal birth defects. You and your husband can try again."

My distraught mother called my father at work, and he immediately made the decision to change doctors. On July 22, 1978, my parents' decision proved God right and a calloused physician wrong. I believe it was nothing more than a satanic attempt to end my life and ministry before it began.

People often ask me when I was called to go into ministry. My answer is, "I cannot remember a moment since I have drawn breath that I didn't want to preach the Word of God." It is just as God told Jeremiah: "Before I formed you in the womb I knew you; before you were born I sanctified you; I ordained you a prophet to the nations" (Jer. 1:5). I believe God did the same for me. That's why there was an attempt on my life in the womb.

Anytime I ask myself, "Has God brought me this far to lose it all?" that moment is one of many in my past that cross my mind. What about you? What has God brought you through that makes you certain beyond a shadow of a doubt, had He not intervened, you would have been destroyed? I assure you, it's not without plan, purpose, and reason. God's plan for your life is not to leave you short of fulfilling your purpose, so you have no reason to worry about the risks involved in making the decision that you face.

Question two

The second question in this pop quiz takes a look ahead and asks, "What will the quality of my life be if I don't even try?"

It is better to try and fail—and try again—than never to try at all. No one can ever answer all the questions that the future holds, but one thing you can know for certain about your future is that if you refuse to try, your quality of life will not improve at all.

Many have stood at this crossroad of risk and reward and wondered what to do. My motto: "If God is for you, who can be against you?"

If the motive for your decision is to fulfill the purpose of God in your life—if the reason for your decision is to benefit others—then the guesswork is done. Go for it! Get out on the edge of the limb where the sweetest fruit is. Enjoy an adventure that will build for you—and those you love—a life and a future of hope and joy in the midst of turmoil and chaos. Lives like this are lived one confident day and one rock-solid decision at a time.

With ordinary talent and extraordinary perse-verance, all things are attainable.[1]

Sir Thomas Foxwell Buxton

PAY THE PRICE OF PERSEVERANCE

My Favorite Olympian

In the summer of 2008, the entire world paused from its unending volatility and struggles and turned its attention to China as that nation hosted its first-ever Summer Olympics. In spite of all that was rumored behind the scenes, without a doubt the ancient civilization did indeed put its best foot forward as it displayed its alluring culture and impressed billions with its modern power and technology. The twenty-ninth Summer Games were certainly something to remember.

As I watched the opening ceremonies with all of its symbolism and stature, I wondered who would be my favorite competitor. Would one of the world's pregame favorites be the one to break records? Would it be an old and familiar face who had made the team out of courtesy but from whom no one expected much? Or would it be some unknown soul who, by the end of the competition, I would never forget? Little did I know that by the end of the games, my favorite Olympian would be someone who wasn't even wearing gold.

David Neville was a track athlete from whom no one expected much. He was a relative newcomer compared to some of the more established and semifamous faces in his event. The four-hundred-meter event was made famous by the unforgettable Michael Johnson, who set world records and raised the bar by taking the gold not only in this event but in the two-hundred-meter event as well.[2]

A number of individuals had shown up in Beijing with the intention of taking Michael's crown as one of the world's greatest runners, and although David Neville probably wouldn't mind the title, he was not someone who even made it on the radar. To be honest, I had no idea who he was until he landed at the finish line in the men's four-hundred-meter final.

I didn't have the chance to keep up with the games as much as I would have liked, and, other than the occasional highlights on the evening news, I hardly watched much of it at all. However, on the evening of the men's four-hundred-meter final, my wife and I had the rare opportunity to sit and visit and watch history in the making halfway around the world. As the race began, all of the commentators were talking about two track stars who had been intense rivals all year long. Everyone expected the two of them to be neck and neck competitors to the end. Another runner from the Bahamas was mentioned as a long shot and a probable third-place finisher.

The tension mounted as the starter gave his final instructions to the runners and the camera panned the waiting racers. Almost as an aside, the announcer stated, "Oh yes, and young David Neville is also an unexpected qualifier for this race and will be starting in lane eight." Other than that, I had never heard of him before.

The gun finally sounded, and, as predicted, the two favorites were well out in front with the young man from the Bahamas playing his role in third. As the world-class sprinters made their way to the finish line, each seemed content to finish where they were. With a combination of exhaustion, agitation, and relief, they each began to pull up as they coasted the last few strides to the finish line.

Everyone, that is, except my favorite Olympian, David Neville. There, in lane number eight, out of nowhere this figure came sailing through the air, stretched out like a flying carpet—not the textbook pose for the finish of a race. Favorites one and two crossed the finish line, gold and silver. But suddenly, a new man was going to finish third.

You guessed it: David Neville. He dived for third as if his life depended on it. When he picked himself up off the ground and discovered that his last-second lunge had won the bronze, he celebrated with the kind of joy that made me believe his life indeed did depend on it! When asked later about his dive, he made two revealing comments: "I did it because it was the only thing I could think to do in the final second," and "God might have pushed me over."[3]

For the first time in a long time, I got emotional watching the Olympics. My wife was looking at me with total confusion, trying to figure out why I was so worked up about third place. I started to realize that what I thought was a lot of hype about the Olympic moment really had more to do with finishing the race strong than it ever did with winning the gold. That victory was much more than just the last spot on the medalist stand. David Neville, whom I have never heard of before, reminded me what it takes to finish—and finish well. His dive for the finish line was not a last-ditch effort for a prize—*it was the flight of perseverance.*

Consider this: For at least the previous four years, if not more, all of his life had gone into preparation for that race. Morning after morning, day after day, he disciplined himself and pushed himself and stressed his physical body to its limit, just to be able to compete. And when the moment came, he would not be denied.

While others were willing to allow all those hours, months, and years of training to end with just coasting in, David chose not to finish in that fashion. He had not come that far to go home empty-handed; he wanted something to show for it.

I so appreciated the expression on his face during the medal ceremony. There on his face was a smile that stretched proudly from ear to ear. In the eyes of some, he had not finished first, but in my eyes, he was, and is, a great champion. He did his best with every ounce of what he had, even if it meant one last lunge of desperation to do it. However brief the moment, David's perseverance put him third in the record books but number one to me.

In Due Season

At some point or another, every life will require perseverance. God in heaven does not require you to finish first, but He does expect you to give it your absolute best all the way to the end. You can rely on any number of resources to take you to the top. Money may provide that opportunity, natural talent and gifts might get you there, or, in some cases, simply good fortune and fate could be given the credit. But no matter how you get to the top, only one thing will keep you there, and that is perseverance.

Perseverance is a unique combination of grit, patience, and effort, which, at times, will require hours of intense endurance and years of patient waiting. Then when put together with moments of extreme effort, it adds up to a powerful resource that will enable you to overcome anything. One who possesses perseverance will remain strong no matter how much the world is shaking.

It has been said, "If it's good, it's worth waiting for." The truth is that if your life is going to attain what you were created for, it will require more than waiting; it's going to take perseverance.

There are a lot of people who have the willingness and desire to try, but few have the ability to persevere. As a society, we are addicted to the instant-gratification mind-set of *right now*. For many of us, any time we are required to wait—much less persevere—we feel as though we are being persecuted. According to the Book of James, this is not persecution. It is the process of our perfection. "Let patience have its perfect work, that you may be perfect and complete, lacking nothing" (James 1:4).

We may put forth the effort to accomplish our goal, but if we do not see the results we want *immediately,* we quit and say, "It's just not meant to be." All too often we forget that the challenges we face did not come to pass overnight, and we have no reason to believe that we can correct them all in a day. Navigating uncertain waters of life will require a number of skills; among them is perseverance.

Perseverance always costs something. There is a phrase in Scripture that I force myself to read on a regular basis. As a matter of fact, every time I come across it, I repeat it over and over again: "In due season." (See Psalm 104:27 and Galatians 6:9 for illustrations of the use of this phrase.) Those three words continually remind me of who I am and the role I am to play.

Psalm 1:3 speaks of the man in a right relationship with God as one who is "like a tree planted by the rivers of water, that brings forth its fruit in *its season*" (emphasis added).

There is nothing instantaneous about a tree. It is the perfect picture of perseverance. It begins in a small and fragile state and must endure the elements of every season—the harsh and bitter cold of the winter, the volatile spring showers and storms, the sweltering dry heat of the summer, and the transition of the fall.

Year after year it continues until finally the season to bear fruit arrives. Then, and only then, will the rewards of perseverance be recognized. This psalm states that a man who is grounded in the Word of God—a source of greatness—is like a tree by a river. When your life is rooted in the foundation of the Word, you have an unending and refreshing source, the kind of source that will give you certainty in uncertain times.

When your source is a river of living water, it will never run dry. You have the strength to endure, the power to produce, and when your appointed time comes, your fruit will be a blessing not only to you but also to those around you, because the end of the verse states, "Whatever he does shall prosper."

> Perseverance is a unique combination of grit, patience, and effort, which, at times, will require hours of intense endurance and years of patient waiting.

I know a lot of people who get really excited about the prosperity portion of the verse, but they often fail to recognize that the key to unlocking the gates of prosperity is perseverance. Galatians 6:9 is another "in due season" verse. It says, "And let us not grow weary while doing good, for in due season we shall reap if we do not lose heart."

I often encounter the "I'll do anything once" syndrome, where people are willing to do something once and then either quit trying or move on. Some apply the "I'll do anything once" principle to their personal lives. For example, they want to lose forty pounds and be in better physical health, so they go to the gym—*once*. They went to the gym for one hour and didn't lose an ounce! So, since they didn't see the results they wanted, they simply refuse to try again. Forget the fact that they continue to pay the membership every month and have hundreds of dollars worth of clothes, shoes, and equipment to convert their physiques into sculpted masterpieces. They tried it once and are not going to try again.

The same is sadly true concerning spiritual perseverance. "I'll pray once..." "I'll participate in worship this one time..." "I'll give my tithes and offering once..." "I'll go to church today and see what happens." Immediately following this first-time experience, they look up at the heavens as if to say, "OK, Lord, I did my part; now do Yours."

Realize that your sporadic behavior doesn't entitle you to God's continual blessings. You are required to persevere, to put forth a consistent effort on a consistent basis. Only through your continual perseverance do you arrive at your "due season" of blessing. Believe me, it's worth the wait.

Perseverance can be a rather overused word, but for the purposes of this chapter, as it relates to a shatterproof life, I offer this definition: "Perseverance is a consistent, high-quality effort in spite of the opposition." When that kind of perseverance describes your life, you will have the assurance that even when your life is shaken, it will not be shattered.

There are some who can perform consistently so long as the conditions are amiable and accommodating. But true perseverance can perform consistently in *any* condition—therein lies the difference.

Business conditions are not nearly as favorable today as they were twenty-four months ago. Perseverance faces the facts and finds a way to keep on performing when others are calling it quits. You may have to redefine your services or scale back to ensure that you are capable of managing your risk, but because you are an individual who is willing to pay the price, you refuse to quit—you persevere and, in due season, overcome.

This kind of perseverance is what makes a marriage the beautiful portrait of love and partnership that God intended it to be. One of the reasons some marriages don't work is because so many people refuse to *work* on their marriage. It's easier to walk away from the difficult moments than to learn how to persevere together. Our society has made divorce a matter of just legal paperwork that can be finalized in a matter of moments. But the truth is that throwing the relationship away because it is convenient for the time being leads to a lifetime of heartache. So what's the answer? Persevere; learn that through true love you can overcome all things, even if it makes you uncomfortable for a while.

Becoming a person of perseverance means that *quit* is not found in your vocabulary. The more the world tries to discourage you, the more you are encouraged to press on. Does that describe you? Can you put out a high-quality effort even when the odds are not in your favor and the world around you is shaking? Or can you only perform when everything is just right?

DISCIPLINE, DUTY, AND DEVOTION

If you are going to develop the ability to persevere, then there are three very real ingredients that you will need in your life: *discipline*, *duty*, and *devotion*. These ingredients are a must in a shatterproof life, and you cannot have one without the others.

When your source is a river of living
water, it will never run dry.

For example, you will never accomplish your duty in life
without discipline, and you will not discipline yourself unless
you are devoted to something greater than you. Let's look at
discipline first.

Discipline

Earlier I mentioned that we are addicted to control. However,
the truth is that of all the things we have learned to control, we
are the one major thing out of control. Our current national
economic crisis is the result of personal spending out of control.
Many of the physical problems we incur in our health are brought
on by personal habits out of control. Often a great number of
the difficulties we endure in our relationships are the result of
personal emotions and responses out of control.

In the previous chapter, I pointed out that it is God who truly
is in control of all things. He is the owner; we are in management.
Since this is the case, *discipline* is how we manage ourselves.
Discipline is the bedrock of perseverance. Without discipline
you may have moments of peak performance and stability, but
you will not be able to maintain it. Your life will be defined by
inconsistency.

Discipline is the dividing wall between the talented and the
tenacious. Talent will indeed take you to the top, but tenacious

discipline will keep you on top. It's the fire that burns in you that cannot be quenched and refuses to let go.

There are a number of talented people in the world, but few have the discipline to manage themselves. How many times have you seen the news report on "Mr. or Mrs. Success" who has fallen from his or her pinnacle of achievement? It happened not because their talents betrayed them but because they betrayed themselves. They had the talent to get there—they just didn't have the discipline to stay there.

Proverbs 25:28 reminds us, "Whoever has no rule over his own spirit is like a city broken down, without walls." Even though there may be tremendous potential and resource in a city, if there are no walls—no control mechanisms—anything and everything goes. Whoever and whatever comes by can have control.

In the same way, a life without discipline has no solid structure, no limit, and no protection against outside influence. Anything can take control. So what's the answer? You must be willing to build discipline in your life in order to maintain control and fulfill your purpose.

Duty

The second aspect of perseverance you must develop in your life is a sense of *duty*. *Duty* is a word that is generally applied to officers who are under authority and are obligated to carry out a task. We often hear about duty in relationship to acts of heroism committed by individuals who did not consider their own well-being but did their duty.

Duty is not what we want to do; it's what we ought to do. If you think you can do your duty without discipline, then good luck. You'll need it. Duty is your service and function in the lives of others.

For example, as a husband and provider, I have a duty to provide for my wife and children. I am held to this obligation not only out of my devotion for them but also out of my commitment to God. He requires it of me just as much as they need it from me. It may not always be easy—there may be moments when quitting looks good—but it's my duty, my service, my purpose, and my obligation. Keeping that in mind will help me through the hard times and give me the self-control to discipline myself to fulfill my responsibility.

A life without discipline has no solid structure, no limit, and no protection against outside influence. Anything can take control.

Samuel, the Old Testament prophet who anointed Saul and David as kings over Israel, understood the meaning of duty. As a prophet, he was responsible to represent the word of the Lord to the people and to represent the people to God.

Before Israel had a king, God was the sovereign ruler of the nation. That meant that when the people wanted to communicate with God, or God had a word for the people, they went and talked to Samuel. This was no small task.

One day the children of Israel decided they were through with this supernatural system of leadership, and they wanted to be like the rest of the natural world and have a king. So, in a sense, they went to Samuel and told him indirectly, "You're fired. We want to have a king like all the other nations." Naturally, this bothered Samuel, so he did what every good prophet should do—he talked to God.

The Lord told Samuel, "Heed the voice of the people...for they have not rejected you, but they have rejected Me" (1 Sam. 8:7). Hagee translation: "Don't worry, Sammy. They didn't fire you; they fired Me!"

I don't know about you, but I am not certain I would have the courage to tell God His people have fired Him! But even more amazing is Samuel's response to the children of Israel. Rather than saying, "Fine. You've fired God. If you're through with Him, then you're through with me, so I'm through with you. Good luck, and good riddance," Samuel told the people, "Moreover, as for me, far be it from me that I should sin against the LORD in ceasing to pray for you" (1 Sam. 12:23).

Samuel refused to be fired. He said, "It's my duty, even if you reject me; I refuse to quit. You didn't appoint me; God did. He has expectations of me that do not change with your opinion. Even if you don't want me, I still have a job to do." That's perseverance; that's discipline; that's greatness in action. That's standing firm and unshakable.

Devotion

The last ingredient required in perseverance is *devotion*. In order to develop the discipline that enables you to do your duty, you need the dedication and loyalty that come from devotion.

In my life there is one woman who captured the essence of

perseverance like none other—my grandmother, Mrs. Vada Hagee. She has been on this earth for ninety-six years and is a living, breathing testament that perseverance does pay off. Her level of self-discipline, her sense of duty, and her devotion to God and family are to me beyond what mere words can describe.

There are a multitude of memories and examples I could share to illustrate my feelings, but for time's sake, I'll limit myself to just one. It concerns her eldest son, Bill. As a child, he was diagnosed with epilepsy, which caused him to have the most violent seizures you could imagine, multiple times a week. At that time, in the late forties and early fifties, medical science offered nothing to alleviate the effects of the condition; it simply gave a lengthy list of all that the patient could not do.

No bike riding—"He may fall." No climbing trees—"He could kill himself." Infrequent trips in public—"His seizures will attract attention and be a source of embarrassment." My grandmother listened to what the doctors had to say and replied, "My child will live a normal life and do what other children do, and if God wants to take him home, that's fine. But he will not be hindered by this disease." Believe me, if you knew my grandmother Vada, you would know she *said* it and *meant* it.

Here is where perseverance comes into play. As a woman of faith, my grandmother, along with my grandfather, stood before their church and prayed for God to heal their son. Had they been "I'll-do-anything-once" Christians, they would have been terribly disappointed because, at that moment, nothing happened. Vada then decided to persevere, and her method of perseverance was to fast. She determined that rather than eat supper with her family, she would prepare the meal, serve the meal, and while her husband and sons ate, she'd go to her bedroom and ask the Lord to heal her son. Her fast was not a two-week experiment of trial and error or a forty-day display. She fasted every night for three straight years!

I am humbled to this very day when I think about the discipline, duty, and devotion it required to do such a feat. As a parent, I realize how precious family time is, and she sacrificed it to go before the Lord on behalf of her oldest boy. For thirty-six months, she carried one request before the Lord: "Heal my son."

> If good things come to those who wait,
> then great things are in store for those
> who are willing to persevere.

It took discipline to do it day in and day out, year after year, and the sense of duty that it was her responsibility to ask God to heal her child. It was devotion that drove her to her knees night after night, asking the Lord just one more time.

I often think about how it felt to go to God in prayer following one of those horrifying seizures. Kneeling by her son as his body shook out of control, she could only comfort him, reassure him that he was all right, help him up, and take him home. Then she had to fix a meal, set the table, and escape to her bedroom to persevere, believing all the while that God would not fail her.

Why did she stop after three years? Because perseverance pays off! One Tuesday evening at their small country church in East Texas, my grandmother was officiating at the service and asked for Bill to come forward and be prayed for. Those who witnessed that night put it this way: "He was instantly healed!" Praise God, he was indeed healed. He is now seventy-three years old and has not had a seizure since the age of sixteen.

However, "instant" does not describe what really happened. His healing actually came after three years of a mother's discipline, duty, and devotion—a mother's perseverance—not giving up until God moved.

I have heard a number of people say, "Your grandmother is a great woman!" I am the first to be in agreement and offer a whole-hearted *amen*! But perseverance was the price she had to pay for the compliment. If good things come to those who wait, then great things are in store for those who are willing to persevere. When it seems like everything in your life is being shaken to the core, apply the quality of perseverance to your situation, and in the end you will not be shattered—you will be victorious.

As is our confidence, so is our capacity.[1]

WILLIAM HAZLITT

EXUDE CONFIDENCE—THE ATTITUDE WITH POTENTIAL

"Mr. Hagee, Would You Hold Me?"

When my father was sixteen years old, he got a job working as the athletic director for the Faith Home Orphanage near his residence in Houston, Texas. The stories he has to share from his days on that campus are always emotionally difficult to hear, but they are a reminder to me of how diffi-cult life can be when your confidence is shaken.

The Faith Home had a policy that if you were no longer able to take care of your child, they would provide care and education at their facility. All you had to do was leave the child at the gate. On many mornings as he walked to work, long before he could see the face, my father heard the sobs of the latest arrival calling for a mother who had left the child there and walked away. He has often described for me the emotional stages that these children went through as they processed the fact that their life had changed forever.

He said, "Son, every orphan has a story." Most of the children would sit up at night and create stories to tell each other about where their parents were, what they were doing, and when they would return to get them. For example: "My father is doing a very important job with the government, something no one else can know about. When he is through, he is going to get a medal from the president, and then he will come back here and get me. We are going to live together on a ranch out west!" One after another, each child created an alternate reality that would distract from the truth.

But each and every Friday these fantasies were destroyed one by one. At the Faith Home, weekend visitation was offered for parents who were in the area to come and pick up their children and spend some time with them over the next few days. Every Friday at 5:00 p.m., the little faces lined up single file and stared straight ahead through the chain-link fence in the hopes that their mothers and fathers would soon be there to get them. They seldom looked at the child standing beside them to their right or left because they didn't want the others to see the doubt and fear in their eyes. Most, if not all, were terribly disappointed when they realized their heroes were not coming, and their make-believe life was shattered by the cold, hard truth. Some would repeat their watch at the fence and keep the vigil week after week, but others soon quit hoping at all and stayed away from the fence, knowing no one would be there.

Soon after these children lost heart, some would withdraw from the world and no longer care to talk to others or be close to anyone. Then there were those who, when it sank in that no one was coming to get them, began to reach out for any figure who cared for them in an attempt to feel normal again.

The self-confidence of each child was shaken to the core. Everything they had believed about their lives was no longer true. They had believed that Mom and Dad would always be there for them, but now they were gone. They had believed they would always have a family; now they had none. They had believed they were going to be taken care of; now they wondered if anyone truly cared. The anchor that had been their foundation became the rock that pulled them under. The source of their stability had failed and was gone, and with it went their confidence.

One morning as my father walked up the drive to the Faith Home, he saw two small boys about six and four years of age standing tied to each other and to the fence where their mother had left them. Attached to the shirt of the oldest was a note that read, "I can no longer afford to feed my sons and myself. Please take care of them; they are good boys."

The four-year-old was already crying, and the six-year-old was doing his best to remain brave. When he saw my father, suddenly he looked up and asked, "Mister, what's your name?"

My father replied, "I am Mr. Hagee."

With one tear falling down his face, he said, "Mr. Hagee, would you please hold me?" In his trembling world, he desperately needed a confident embrace.

No one can thrive without confidence. It is the attitude that maximizes potential and enables you to reach the ultimate goals of your life. Confidence comes from knowing who you are and where you came from. It gives the strength and determination that you need to establish proper priorities, make good decisions, and develop the determination that is required to persevere.

The world is full of people who have been

shaken by the unexpected events of life, which have left them searching for confidence they can embrace. When you know where your confidence comes from, no matter how unstable things in the world may get, you will always remain rock solid and secure.

What Do You Do When Things Go Wrong?

"Catch me, Daddy" is a phrase I often get to hear these days. My daughter, Hannah, and my son, John William, are at the ages where children love to test their limits. They call, "Catch me," as they jump from the base of the stairs or from the side of the pool or from any other height they have recently conquered.

The other day, we were in the backyard when both children climbed onto the ledge of my patio, which is about two and a half feet off the ground. At this moment, they synchronized their departures with the famous phrase "Catch me, Daddy!"

There I was with two children flying at me from different directions and hardly a moment to react. The outcome brought mixed reviews; I was able to reach out and grab John William, my two-year-old, in mid flight, but I barely had time to break the fall for Hannah, my four-year-old, as she hit the ground.

My son thought it was a trip and couldn't wait to do it again. My daughter's eyes got big as she welled up with tears and immediately wanted to know why I had let her down. "Why did you drop me?" she asked over and over. She proceeded to tell my wife over and over, "Daddy dropped me," which created a whole different level of explanation.

Now, rather than climbing up and saying, "Catch me, Daddy," her new phrase is, "Don't drop me, Daddy." Her confidence in me is a bit shaken. What she thought would happen did not happen, and this unexpected outcome gave her a whole new perspective.

What happens to you when things don't turn out as you thought they should? In many ways, life can cause you to experience the same emotions my daughter did when she hit the ground. The outcome will cause your confidence and trust to be a bit shaken. You may be willing to try again, but now there's an element of doubt and fear as to what you think the outcome might be.

Suddenly you begin to behave in a more guarded manner. Rather than make a decision and go for it, your apprehension creates an uncertainty that impacts everything you do. This new outlook can truly be a major setback to living up to your full potential and in extreme cases can redefine you. After all, you don't want to get hurt again or to be let down and disappointed again. You don't want to suffer the pain of failure again, and in an effort to avoid such pain, you lose your identity.

Before you allow life to steal your confidence, you must answer this question: How can I expect to be successful when I don't expect anything good to happen to me?

People who successfully endure through the most difficult times have an attitude of confidence that impacts everything they do. Where does that kind of confidence come from? How can you get hold of it in your life? Before we go any further, we must first define what living with confidence truly means.

LIVING A LIFE OF FAITH

Living with confidence means living a life of faith. Confidence is actually translated from two Latin words put together to make one word. The first part is *con*, which means "with"; the second part is *fidio*, which means "faith." Therefore, *being confident* means to live with faith.

Some live with faith in self, others put their faith in education and intellect, and some have faith in financial resources and wealth. If these are the sources of your confidence, you need to know that sooner or later your faith will be shaken if not shattered. If you want to thrive while others struggle, *then your confidence and faith can only be found one place, and that place is in God.* All other resources may fail, but God has never failed.

The way to live with confidence in your life is to rediscover your true identity, which the circumstances of your life will try to steal. Like my little daughter, who thought I would be there to catch her, perhaps your faith has been shaken and you have gone from speaking with confidence and anticipation, "Catch me," to being filled with fear and shouting, "Don't drop me!"

The young man my father met at the gate that morning in Houston had reached a time when he just needed to be embraced—and it didn't matter from whom. You may find yourself at that same point. Every unexpected turn of events in one way or another will create a series of questions, and those questions cause you to tremble to the point that you'll cling to anything.

It's the way you answer those difficult questions that determines whether you press on or quit altogether. When your source of confidence in uncertain times is found in the assurance of who God is, then no matter the size of the question, you will always have an almighty answer. This kind of answer will always remind you of the person He created you to be, and it will never let you lose sight of your identity no matter how much your world is shaking.

Life has a way of stealing identity. For some, it happens early with a deep emotional trauma suffered in childhood, a divorce that divides your family, or a relationship that turns abusive.

Failure has a way of stealing your identity too, whether it's personal or professional. Failure can cause people to wonder if they will ever succeed again. There are times when people set unrealistic goals for themselves, and no matter how high their level of achievement, they feel they have fallen short and have not achieved much at all. No matter what the cause, the result is a lack of confidence, and somewhere along life's road, you simply forgot who you used to be.

If you want to thrive while others struggle, *then your confidence and faith can only be found one place, and that place is in God.*

I have seen this "emotional identity theft" change people so much that they lose confidence in their ability to make simple decisions. Life just hangs in a stalemate as they wonder what to do next. Some lose hope that anything good will ever happen in their lives, to the point they can no longer distinguish the good from the bad. Everything starts to look and feel the same: *hopeless.*

Others find it difficult to trust anyone and are often suspicious that others are working against them instead of looking out for them. If any of this describes you, you are in good company. There have been plenty of truly great people right where you are, and God still used them mightily. They went through tremendous times of physical, emotional, and spiritual shaking but through it all remained unshattered.

I'll Never Do That Again

Of all the figures who have graced the stage of human history, I can find none greater to use as an example than Moses. Moses suffered from a severe lack of confidence due to a case of emotional identity theft. In order to grasp how deep Moses had buried his true self, you must compare a lesser-known description of him found in Acts 7:20–25 with the man we see making excuses in Exodus 3.

When we pick up the story of Moses in Exodus 3, he is arguing with God. We can read his arguments in Exodus 3:11–4:17. He asks:

- "Who am I?"
- "What shall I say?"

- "What if they don't believe me or listen to my voice?"
- "What if they doubt?"
- "Can't You send someone else?"

If I thought that way before I went to the pulpit on Sunday, I wouldn't be able to give my name and address. In Exodus 4:10 we begin to see the truth shining through about Moses's lack of confidence. He says:

> Then Moses said to the LORD, "O my Lord, I am not eloquent, neither before nor since You have spoken to Your servant."

Here is where we must read the seventh chapter of Acts to see who Moses was before he left Egypt. He, indeed, was at one time eloquent and able to achieve at the highest level. When he was living in Egypt, he was living with confidence and faith in himself. His education is described this way: "Moses was learned in all the wisdom of the Egyptians, and was mighty in words and deeds" (Acts 7:22). His resources were plentiful; he was raised as royalty—as a prince in Egypt—by Pharaoh's daughter (v. 21). As a matter of fact, he was confident, educated, and mighty in words and deeds. He was not some ignorant and crude shepherd—even though he sounds like one in Exodus 3–4.

So, what's the problem? What made Moses change?

We discover in the seventh chapter of Acts that Moses's faith was badly shaken. He had placed all of his faith in himself—all that he thought he was capable of and what he thought he had the power to do. This fact caused him to take matters into his own hands and to murder an Egyptian whom he saw beating an Israelite slave (Acts 7:24).

Moses walked away from this act of violence and thought, "My, what a great job I did! You know, I bet all the Israelites in Egypt will really appreciate me for this. After all, they've been marching in brick pits for four hundred years, and I have been raised like royalty. So, killing one Egyptian is going to make it all better, right?"

Wrong!

The next day Moses took a stroll through the pits and saw two Israelis fighting. He decided to intervene, and they ate his lunch. "Who do you think you are, rich boy?" Actually, they said, "Who made you a ruler and a judge over us? Do you want to kill me as you did the Egyptian yesterday?" (vv. 27–28).

Life has a way of stealing identity.

With those words, a wave of fear crashed over Moses. As fast as his feet could carry him, he ran away from all that he had placed his faith and confidence in, away from his position in the royal family, away from his education and influence, away from his wealth and power. With every step he took toward the desert, he distanced himself farther and farther from who he used to be. He lost all confidence in who he was altogether. Life's unexpected response stole Moses's identity.

By the time we meet him again forty years later, when Moses had had his famous conversation with the voice in the burning bush, you didn't hear a man mighty in words and deeds—you heard a man who was terrified to try again. He had one excuse after another as to why he was the wrong guy. Finally, he told God, "O my Lord, please send by the hand of whomever else You may send" (Exod. 4:13). Moses was a victim of identity theft.

If you walked into Jethro's camp with Acts 7 as your personality profile for Moses, Jethro would tell you, "There is a man who lives here by that name, but he certainly does not fit the description." He might say, "Our Moses is pretty quiet. He has been known to stutter a little bit. He's pretty content to watch the sheep and carry his staff. If he has any super secrets from the brightest minds in Egypt, he certainly hasn't shared them with us."

You might respond: "But the profile I am reading says he is 'mighty in words and deeds'" (Acts 7:22).

Jethro's reply would most likely be, "Hmmm, you may be talking about *a* Moses, but I don't think that you are looking for our Moses; they're just not the same person."

What was the problem? Moses allowed his failure to redefine him. Have you? Have you stopped living with confidence and faith? You cannot allow the setbacks of yesterday and the difficulties of today to steal your identity; you must not allow failure to redefine you. *You* must redefine failure.

Failure does not need to be the end of the journey where all hope is lost. Failure is nothing more than the end of one opportunity and the beginning of the next. I remember reading an interview about Thomas Edison, the inventor of the light bulb. He was asked about his repeated attempts to create the light bulb, and he gave this answer: "I have not failed. I've just found ten thousand ways that won't work."[2]

What a profound perspective on what some would have defined as failure. Edison knew what his goal was, and he would not allow a few missed steps to deter him from his purpose. He simply considered them one step closer to the prize.

THE ATTITUDE WITH POTENTIAL

So, how do you get your confidence back? Look at the rest of the conversation between Moses and the Lord at the burning bush. In spite of all the excuses Moses gave, God reassured Moses over and over again: "I will go with you." "I Am has sent you."

The message to Moses was pretty simple. Jehovah God was telling Moses, "The last time you tried this, it was with confidence in you and you alone. This time it will be with confidence in Me and Me alone."

The first time Moses walked the streets of Egypt, his faith was in the limited ability he possessed. This time he walked into Pharaoh's courtroom with his faith in the unlimited power of the Almighty. With a staff in his hand and God in his heart, Moses possessed an attitude with the confidence to change the world. He was back in touch with his source. He had his priorities in the right place, and, at the age of eighty, Moses began to make decisions that would lead him to his destiny. It's truly never too late to start living up to your full potential.

Failure is nothing more than the
end of one opportunity and the
beginning of the next.

You may feel like you don't have what it takes to do what
Moses did. I assure you, you do. You came from the same source
he came from. The same God who had a plan and a destiny for
Moses has a plan and a destiny for you. Although there are a lot
of potential excuses you might make, I assure you that God has
already taken all of that into account, and His grace is sufficient
to compensate for your every need.

You may lack the confidence, but you do not lack the resources
so long as God is with you. All Moses had was a staff; however,
the supernatural power of God made that staff no ordinary stick.
It may have been all that was in his hand and all that he had to
give, but it was more than enough to do the job. Have enough
faith in God to put what you hold in your hand into His, and
see what He does with it. When you do, you'll develop a sense of
true confidence and attitude with real potential.

There is no poverty that can overtake diligence.

JAPANESE PROVERB

Managing Your Resources
With Diligence

What Can You Get for Two Dollars?

When my father gave his heart to the Lord in January 1958, he felt led of God to enter the ministry, and within a week, he enrolled at the Southwestern Bible Institute in Waxahachie, Texas. It is now known as Southwestern Assemblies of God University.

On the day he left home, his parents emptied their savings of the seventy-five dollars in the account and informed their son that when the seventy-five dollars was gone, they would not be able to continue supporting him. In those days, students were allowed to pay tuition on a six-week basis. The money given to my father enabled him to pay for the first six weeks of school and enough bologna and cheese not to starve until other arrangements could be made. My father knew he needed a job, and he needed one quickly.

It just so happened that the best job in town was the only job in town—working in the church furniture factory—and there was a waiting list prioritized from the upperclassmen on down for a spot. My freshman father had little chance, if any, of getting hired, but he figured it never hurt to ask. Of course, he was turned down; they were not hiring, and he was not even on the waiting list.

Week one turned into week two, which quickly became three. The meager funds were dwindling, and the church furniture factory was still not hiring. My father, in spite of the furniture factory foreman's standard reply, persisted in asking every week, "You guys hiring?" and every time received the same answer: "No!"

Even as the seemingly inevitable end was drawing near, my father continued to make plans for his future. If the situation didn't change, he had made up his mind that he had no choice but to join the army; after all, there was nothing to go back home to. The sixth and final week arrived, and still there was no job and no answer in sight.

The last weekend came before my father would have to report to the admissions office on Monday to withdraw. He spent that Saturday washing cars in the bitter North Texas cold for a meager fifty cents an hour. February is no time to wash cars, much less work outside in Waxahachie. He has shared many times with me that it was the hardest two dollars he had ever earned.

After going back to the dorm, changing his clothes, packing his things, and making preparations to leave, he stopped by the campus chapel to hear Charles Greenaway fresh from the mission field of Africa. The missionary showed slides of the people to whom he had been ministering, describing their great need and how very little they really had. As the service continued, the Lord began to move on my father to give all that he had earned that cold winter day.

I assure you, a brief and intense discussion ensued between God and my father!

"It's all I have!"

"Give it."

"It is all I have!"

"Give it."

"It is *ALL I HAVE!*"

"GIVE IT!"

The moment of truth arrived, and my father obeyed. I've heard him say he squeezed those two bills until the ink stained his fingers. Without a doubt, they were hard to let go.

At a moment like this, you would expect the testimony to end with the heavens opening, angels singing, and a mighty voice from heaven saying something deep and affirming, but none of that happened. John Hagee went back to his dorm flat broke and feeling sick. He still had no answers to the challenges he faced. He could not afford to stay in school, and there was no place for him to go but straight into the military.

Sunday came and went, and nothing changed. Monday morning rolled around, and on his way to inform the school he had to leave, he decided to stop by the furniture factory one more time. "You know, I thought I would stop by and give you guys one more chance to hire me!" he said with a mischievous grin.

The factory manager smiled and responded by saying, "This morning I had a senior quit, and I have never seen anyone who is as determined and diligent as you. When can you start?" Dad refused to change his clothes or to leave the man's side. He put on a carpentry apron and went straight to work. The income from the job would at least keep him in school if it did nothing else.

What I am about to tell you is fifty years of ministerial history in a few short lines. A couple of weeks after his new occupation began, John Hagee was asked to go to the pulpit for the first time. He shared a message with a youth group at a small church in Dallas. That night, the senior pastor stopped by the service and heard what my father had to say. At the close of the service, he extended an invitation for the same message to be shared with his congregation the next Sunday morning.

Dad accepted the opportunity, fully expecting for this to be one service and one service only. During the invitation, a number of people made decisions to surrender their lives to Christ, and in classic Pentecostal fashion, a revival was born.

Every night for three weeks, Dad would finish his schoolwork, go to the furniture factory, work until closing, shower, change, and drive to Dallas for the evening service. At the end of the third week, he was so tired he informed the pastor, "You can do what you want tomorrow night, but I am too tired to come."

That night the small Dallas church took a love offering for their young guest speaker and sent him home with three hundred dollars! It was a far cry from where he was just a few weeks earlier with only two dollars to his name. With his small fortune, my father felt he could make a down payment on the world!

The story doesn't end there of course. The pastor who invited my father to speak at his church also extended to him an invitation to preach at a pastors' sectional rally a few weeks later. At that event, an eighteen-year-old John Hagee stood in the pulpit—a young unknown preacher with a lot of potential—and walked away with eighteen months' worth of speaking engagements.

Bible school was more than paid for. The bologna and cheese was exchanged for hot meals in the cafeteria, and every need he had for the duration of his ministry training was met.

Fifty-one years later, John Hagee Ministries has a media presence in every nation of the world. God has been faithful to provide more than we can contain along the way. The lessons learned early in a young minister's career are still serving him well today. Obedience to God and a diligent work ethic are the cornerstones of an unshakable way to manage your finances—and your life.

Now, can you tell me where else but from God you can get all of that for just two dollars?

WHO'S IN CHARGE OF THE CHECKBOOK?

The principles you read in chapter 4—discipline, duty, and devotion—need to be very real ingredients in your life before any of the economic truths in this chapter can take effect.

The major issue regarding money that always needs to be resolved is determining *who's in charge*. Almost every economic battle I have ever observed on any level is about control.

When two companies place their products next to each other on the shelf, they are fighting for control of the market. When the representatives and elected officials of our government meet with the power players of the world, it's about who controls the trade, commerce, and treasury.

They may use fancy words like *stimulus*, *development*, and *bailout*, but the truth is that it's not about assistance and aid—it's about control.

Consider most of the arguments that have taken place in your home on the topic of money and finance. The discussion is not really about what you can and cannot afford or what you want to buy and your spouse doesn't want to buy. It's about who has control of the checkbook. Who's in charge of the dollars in your house?

All of my life, my father has told me, "Son, you will either master money, or money will master you." If you are not obediently and diligently managing your finances, you will discover that economic chaos results, which is the opposite of control. It will be the kind of chaos that has credit card companies enjoying more of your paycheck than you do. Such chaos does not reflect the biblical definition of success, and yet it seems to define most *successful* Americans today.

Think about my father's brief yet intense dialogue with God in the college chapel that evening. Two dollars was not going to get him a bus ticket out of town, but since it was all he had, he didn't want to lose control of it. Had he kept what he had and remained in control, I do not know where he would be today. Because he was willing to be obedient and let go, I can tell you that where God has taken him has been nothing short of miraculous.

Remember this: *We control nothing.* We are here in the position of management. To pretend that we are the owners disconnects us from God and sends us headfirst on a collision course with God our provider. We are not here to be in control of money; we are here to manage it.

This is why the day I left home for the university I determined to pursue a degree in business. I already had a theology professor at home in my father, and he could teach me everything I would require for ministry. But what I truly needed was the understanding of how to manage money. From the looks of our current economic crisis, there are plenty of people in the world who could use a few lessons in money management.

Money is sometimes treated like a forbidden topic. People often preface the subject with the phrase "If you don't mind me asking..." Then they inquire, "How much...?" or "What did you...?" or "Could you tell me...?" as if the financially based question they are about to ask is offensive, inappropriate, and off-limits. Treating the topic of money in such a fashion is absurd. No matter who you are or what you do, if you are compensated for services rendered in our modern world, the form of compensation is money.

To illustrate the point further, I have a line of young people at my office door every spring seeking my counsel on their education. They want to know: "What degree should I pursue?" "What school should I attend?" After they fill me in on all of their exciting plans for the future, I ask this question: "What courses do you plan to take on the subject of money and finance?"

"Oh, well, Pastor Matt, you don't understand. I'm going to be a doctor...biologist...engineer...journalist...veterinarian, and so forth." The list goes on and on.

My reply to their rebuttal is always the same: "And when you get paid for doing what you went to school to learn to do, how will they pay you?"

"Money."

"And what will you do with that money once they pay you?"

This answer always varies from "Ummm" to "Well..." or a flat-out "I don't know."

The entire wealth-management industry is built on this one fact: people know how to *make* money, but few know how to *manage* it.

So many people are well educated and informed on many topics but absolutely in the dark on the subject of money. This needs to change...soon.

Resource Management

When it comes to your finances, you indeed have a role to play, but it must be within proper relationship to your Father in heaven, the provider of all things. In order for this to occur, you need to understand God's economic system and where you fit in.

God Himself wants you to be His resource manager here on Earth. As His manager, you do what He instructs you to do because He is the owner. To those who prove themselves capable in this area, the Lord extends the promise found in Deuteronomy 28:13: "And the Lord will make you the head and not the tail; you shall be above only, and not be beneath." This verse has nothing to do with placement; it has to do with who is calling the shots. If you are the head, you are in charge, and that's right where the Lord wants you to be economically—in charge. So how do you get there?

First, you must put everything in its proper place. Remember, you are not the source; God is. You are His steward. The definition of a *steward* is a fiscal agent who manages the resources and provisions of his master. That's what God wants you to be for Him here on Earth, His steward.

I remember the first time that my family went on a cruise. On the first day we arrived on board, a man graciously introduced himself to us as our cabin steward. For the next seven days, I am not sure if he slept, or where he slept, but every time we turned around, he was there.

If we left the room for five minutes, he would sneak in somehow, some way, and tidy up. We never found his secret entrance, but he was amazing; he missed nothing! Throughout our entire trip, we didn't have to ask for a thing. It was as if he was reading our minds, and everything that we could have asked for was already in place before we even thought to ask.

He was diligently managing the resources of that cabin, and we were, indeed, the beneficiaries of his tireless effort. Every time I study the topic of stewardship I think about him and how God expects the same performance from me concerning what He has entrusted into my hand.

There are people who get nervous every time you mention God and money in the same sentence. However, to be fair, you cannot have a meaningful conversation about money without God in it. Haggai 2:8 declares, "'The silver is Mine, and the gold is Mine,' says the LORD of hosts." So, when you are talking about money, you're talking about what already belongs to Him anyway. After all, He gave you the power and strength to obtain it: "And you shall remember the LORD your God, for it is He who gives you power to get wealth" (Deut. 8:18).

Remember this: *We control nothing.*
We are here in the
position of management.

So, if God gave you the power to get it and then allowed you to have it, don't you think it's fair that when we discuss it we include Him too? Let me put it this way: He owns it all and has entrusted it to your care. The most important question you can answer is "How well am I managing the Master's resources?"

Personally, that question excites me. To think I am the resource manager for the One who owns the cattle on a thousand hilltops, buried every precious stone, and possesses all the silver and all the gold. Wow, what a job!

When you absorb that principle, you will begin to see that it really doesn't matter what's taking place in the world around you. You can succeed in any economic environment because God is the source behind your income. When you manage it the way He desires, He personally sees to it that you receive more of it.

> "And try Me now in this," says the LORD of hosts, "if I will not open for you the windows of heaven and pour out for you such blessing that there will not be room enough to receive it."
>
> —MALACHI 3:10

When you have more than you can receive, you can build a stable economic foundation that can endure any amount of financial uncertainty.

Before this economic strong tower becomes your reality, you have to abandon all of your man-made economic theories and wrap your mind around God's economic law. Man has many theories. There is communism, which says the state owns it all. There is capitalism, which says the citizen owns it all, and there are a number of other theories in between, each with its own nuances. The truth is there is only one economic law you need to memorize, and it is the economic law of the kingdom. That law states that God owns it all.

When you recognize this truth, you will find great joy in doing what He wants you to do with the resources He gives you. "God loves a cheerful giver" (2 Cor. 9:7). A person can give cheerfully when he or she fully understands where all their resources come from and what the purpose is behind them.

God's primary purpose for His resources in your life is to get them *through* you, not *to* you. You are not to be a collection agency; you ought to be a distribution center. The more God sees you distributing, the more He is willing to send to you because He knows you will do what He requires of you.

"Give, and it will be given to you" (Luke 6:38). The text goes on to say that with the same volume you pour it out, God will pour it in. If you give in droplets, He'll give in droplets. Likewise, if you give in buckets, He'll give in buckets. The more God sees you distributing His resources, the more trust He develops in you as His steward.

A NEED-MEETING GOD

Understand that God is in the *need-meeting business*. He has repeatedly promised His children that He will provide for their every need. God particularly likes to use us as His agents to accomplish this task. When we respond in obedience in our financial lives by distributing His resources to help meet the needs of others, He personally sees to it that our needs are met.

Consider the account in 1 Kings 17:8–16. The world was in a season of economic shaking, and God sent His prophet Elijah into the house of a single mother who was preparing her last meal for her only child. Elijah had the nerve to ask this woman for her last bite of bread, and, shockingly, she gave it to him.

At a time when the world was falling apart and conventional wisdom and maternal instinct would have said, "Get all you can, and can all you get," she fed this hungry preacher her last tortilla, and he willingly ate it. Now, of course, we have the benefit of the rest of the story.

The woman's barrel of meal was miraculously replenished, and her vessel of oil did not run dry. She, her son, and Elijah were supernaturally provided for while the rest of the world starved and suffered through a famine. Why? It was because this woman was willing to be obedient and diligent with the resources God entrusted to her.

God's primary purpose for His resources in your life is to get them *through* you, not *to* you.

In the theater of my mind, I can see her kneeling by her son's bed at night to pray, knowing that her barrel will soon be empty and her oil will run dry. When she ran out of food, there would be nothing left to do but die. I can hear her anxious plea: "God, please help me. If You don't make a way for us to eat, we are going to starve to death. My baby is hungry and deserves better, but I am doing the best I can do with what I've got. I need You to help me do the rest."

I know that in a million years she would have never expected God's answer to show up in the belly of a hungry preacher, but His ways are not our ways. The moment she gave what she had, her Provider in heaven gave more than she ever imagined. She was shaken but not shattered. She was hungry, but she didn't starve to death. She made a sacrifice and was rewarded with more than enough to meet her needs.

Of all the principles locked within this illustration, there is one that stands out above the rest. When it comes to giving, God measures the weight of the sacrifice—not the size of the check.

I am always appalled when some billion-dollar organization gets front-page news for the few hundred thousand dollars they gave away. Don't get me wrong; the moment was nice for the recipient, I'm sure. But most of the time, their meager check didn't mean all that much in comparison to *what they could have done.*

When the word *give* is translated into Hebrew, one of the synonyms that you will find is the word *pain.* Why? Because in certain cultures, it's not considered giving until it hurts. Without a doubt it was a painful thing for the widow in Zarephath to fix the meal for Elijah and watch him eat it. You just know she must have had a terrible lump in her throat when she poured out the last drop of what she had. She must have been thinking, "There it goes; what's next?" Remember, however, that it was the size of her sacrifice, not the amount she gave, that mattered.

Then there is the widow in the New Testament who had the courage to give when others thought that it wouldn't count for much at all. (See Mark 12:41–44.) Jesus and His disciples were in the temple as people were walking forward to present their offerings to the Lord. Jesus watched as the *parade of pride* marched up the aisle—one pompous Pharisee after another presenting their *gifts* to the Lord. Religion has a way of making people think they are important.

Then comes a meager figure—not at all dressed like the others—with no air of egotistical arrogance like those by whom she is surrounded. You might have expected her to *ask for alms* rather than give anything at all. Yet she sows with the others as if she fits right in. All she gave were two small mites, the lowest form of currency available. Put them together, and they were worth less than the penny you stepped over and ignored on the sidewalk.

In the midst of her sacrifice, Christ pointed out this truth to His disciples: "Assuredly, I say to you that this poor widow has put in more than all those who have given to the treasury; for they all put in out of their abundance, but she out of her poverty put in all that she had, her whole livelihood" (Mark 12:43–44).

It is not the size of the check; it is the place from which it comes. When you give, do you give out of your heart or out of your coin purse? What you do may impress others, but until you give from the heart, you will not impress God.

How Much Is Too Much?

God's economy is *need driven*, not *greed driven*. People sometimes develop a false sense of guilt when it comes to their material possessions because they attempt to apply man's perspective to God's economic system. The first thing you need to know about the amount of money that you have is that you will never have enough to impress God. He has yet to look at the bottom line on a balance sheet and marvel. God is not concerned with how much you have, but He is concerned with how you manage it.

Look at Solomon. He had so much that he used gold for the hinges on the gates of his horse stables. Did God have a problem with it? Absolutely not. He uses gold for asphalt. While it's true that Solomon had some fine things in his palace and throne room, he also spared no expense when building a house for God. As a matter of fact, Solomon asserted, "And the temple which I build will be great, for our God is greater than all gods" (2 Chron. 2:5). The point is that Solomon was a giver.

When it comes to giving, God measures
the weight of the sacrifice—not the size
of the check.

When God sees that you are willing to meet needs with the resources He gives you, you will receive more. Remember the biblical equation I mentioned earlier? The more needs you meet, the more blessings you will receive. God's perspective on prosperity is that you should have enough to meet your needs and some left over to give.

If you are asking God for ten million dollars, the question you must be prepared to answer is: Do you have a ten-million-dollar need? If the answer to this question is no, then your desire to obtain the amount has nothing to do with God's financial purpose for your life.

Don't forget this fact: God delights Himself in your prosperity. He loves to see you doing well and enjoying the best of things, but He wants to make sure you are operating from a need basis and not a greed basis. You may possess what the world around you considers a fortune, and then again, you may have just enough to get by. It's not the amount that matters; it's what you do with it that counts.

How Should I Give?

When it comes to giving and stewardship, God has a certain formula for how He wants you to give. First, He wants you to give to Him. The Bible calls this "firstfruits." There are a number of teachings on the topic, and my purpose is not to reiterate them here. The thing you need to know about firstfruits is that the moment you give to God, His blessings come upon everything else you possess. Therefore, wouldn't it make more sense to give to God first so that His blessings are upon what remains?

When the last person on your giving list is God, what's left for Him to place His blessing upon? I have heard it said this way: "When you give God your leftovers, He gives you His."

The next place God wants you to give is to His house. "Bring all the tithes into the storehouse, that there may be food in My house" (Mal. 3:10). After you have given your firstfruits, God wants you to give an offering—not to an individual, but to His house. Why?

There are people who argue, "If I know someone who has a need and I give directly to that person, am I not doing the right thing?" I don't know; are you? Let me give you a spiritual litmus test that will never give you inaccurate results.

If what you are doing is done out of a pure heart and for the right reason, then it will glorify God—not you. If you are giving to gratify yourself, then you need to be aware of the problems that can result from such behavior.

When you give directly to someone and you receive the glory, then you become the provider. God says, "So you think you can do My job; good luck!" In this case, the recipient will sing your praises for the momentary relief that you brought in his or her hour of crisis. But since you have trained them to turn to you and not to their true provider, then this is only the beginning of the long list of problems you will get the chance to solve. Sooner or later, your resources will no longer be enough, and then where will you turn?

The second issue that can arise with this behavior is that you may be *enabling* this person, not *empowering* him or her. God's resources are intended to empower people to do His will, not to enable them with a handout. The Word is very clear on this point: "If anyone will not work, neither shall he eat" (2 Thess. 3:10). Handouts improperly train people to think that they are entitled to resources that are not theirs and that they did not earn. Even in the Old Testament, the Lord always arranged for resources to be set aside for the needy, but they had to work in order to obtain them.

This is illustrated in the story of God sending manna for the children of Israel in the wilderness. They didn't prepare the meal; God did, but they still had to go pick it up.

In the Book of Ruth, you read that Ruth was picking up wheat from the corners of Boaz's field. The Word of God forbade a landowner from cutting the corners of his field during the harvest. He had to leave it for the needy and the poor to come and gather what they needed to carry home and eat. They may not have owned what they were picking, but they still had to put in some effort to obtain it.

When you see the need of an individual, at times it is appropriate to give directly to that need. However, when you are giving to a Bible-based church that manages its resources by the Word of God, that church will be there to meet that need, and the glory will go to whom it belongs—God. He will see that your obedience to His Word is rewarded.

For example, at Cornerstone Church in San Antonio, Texas, we have an entire department set aside for benevolence. The faithful members of the congregation support it with their offerings, and it is intended to be available to help those in need.

One of the major responsibilities within the department is to identify what caused the need in the first place and then to determine a course of action that will solve the problem permanently. The assistance given is intended to empower the recipient to overcome his or her setback—not to subsidize that person's lack.

If you want God's favor on your finances, the best thing you can do is invest them in places where He will have the opportunity to create a return on your investment. I know what you are thinking: "What do you mean, return on investment?" To put it simply, when you give to God, He gives back to you. On Wall Street that is called receiving *a return on your investment*.

I love the fact that when you properly manage God's resources, He begins to manage your portfolio. Organizations like churches and ministries that are preaching the gospel, feeding the hungry, helping the homeless, and allowing the light of the love of God to shine through them are great places to make an investment. Wherever you choose to give, be sure you see that the practical and spiritual needs of others are being met. Then you will gain God's favor in your finances.

TAKE CARE OF YOURSELF

Not only does God expect you to be a giver and a worker, but He expects you to be a steward of your physical body as well.

As a steward, not only are you in charge of God's financial resources, but you are also in charge of His physical resources, beginning with you. The Bible says that you are the temple of the very Spirit of God. You will never achieve your purpose financially or spiritually if you do not take care of yourself physically.

If you want to see this principle of stewardship in action in a life that was shaken but not shattered, look at Joseph. No matter where he was, he made it a point to do his job with all of his heart to the best of his ability. This willingness to do his best no matter what the circumstance caused him to be placed in control wherever he went. In Potiphar's estate, he was placed in charge of every square inch of property. In prison, he was the head trustee. When he found himself in front of Pharaoh, rather than start spewing venom about all the injustice he had suffered, he interpreted a dream about stewardship.

Then he told Pharaoh how to manage the resources of the entire kingdom in order to save the whole world. (See Genesis 41.) "For seven years we should set some aside, and for seven years we should use what we've set aside to sell to the world." This guy was good! Pharaoh was so impressed with what he heard that he said, "Joseph, my man, you're in charge."

> If you want God's favor on your finances, the best thing you can do is invest them in places where He will have the opportunity to create a return on your investment.

When Joseph's family showed up, he had more than enough food to meet their physical needs. He provided them with the choice land of Goshen for their flocks and herds, and he was in enough control of his heart, soul, mind, and body that he was able to embrace them and say, "You meant evil against me; but God meant it for good" (Gen. 50:20).

When you properly utilize the resources God has given you, both physically and financially, God puts you in control. When you're in control—above and not beneath, the first and not the last, the head and not the tail—your economic outlook will be unshakable.

No man, for any considerable period, can wear one face to himself and another to the multitude.[1]

NATHANIEL HAWTHORNE

BE IDENTIFIED BY YOUR INTEGRITY

Sir Winston, Where Are You?

To me, no other historical figure is more distinguish-

able in the modern era than Sir Winston Churchill.

Even those who are unfamiliar with his story and the

great leadership he provided to the world in an hour

of crisis can clearly identify him in the pictures of

history books and museums that cover the four cor-

ners of civilization where he left his indelible mark.

In the current trembling and quaking world we live in, one might faintly wonder, "Sir Winston, where are you now when we need you so very badly?"

The more you learn about Winston Churchill, the more you discover that while he may still be revered at the highest levels, it is for certain that he also possessed certain qualities that made him far less than a saint. His quick wit and sharp tongue put him in a league all his own, both as an orator and individual. His speeches to England and the rest of the world brought glimmers of hope in terribly dark hours, and his willingness to bluntly address the most difficult and delicate subjects made him invaluable at the time when he served his generation.

Some of my fondest Churchill moments come from outside of his role as prime minister and politics and are quotes from his personal life. I have often quoted his response to Lady Astor, who despised Winston's unchaste behavior. In one of their more famous arguments, Lady Astor was quoted as saying, "If I were married to you, I'd put poison in your coffee."

To which he quickly responded, "If I were married to you, I'd drink it."[2]

In his boldness he may have come across as offensive at times; however, you never had to guess where he stood. You may have disapproved, but you could at least respect his position because there was no doubt as to where he had drawn the line.

To me, Sir Winston Churchill, in spite of his humanistic shortcomings, was a man of great integrity. His possessed the kind of integrity that will get you through tough times, the kind that is transparent and says, "Like it or not, here is the truth." It was the kind of integrity that, unfortunately, you do not encounter these days, at a time when we so desperately need it.

Churchill's integrity did not come from prudence and manners. It came from genuine sincerity that was willing to take on any task. Winston was a man with nothing to hide, even if you didn't want to see what he was willing to expose. This next illustration may give you some more insight into exactly what I mean.

On his first trip to Washington DC to meet with President Franklin D. Roosevelt, Churchill was caught off guard when the president came to his room unexpectedly after his morning bath. There, with the president of the United States staring at his naked body, rather than running from the awkward and embarrassing moment, Churchill said, "Please come in, Mr. President. His Majesty's first minister has nothing to hide from the president of the United States."

As funny as it may seem, integrity is when you

have nothing to hide—no matter how good, bad, or ugly. I really do wish there were more people like that still around.

WHAT IS INTEGRITY, AND WHERE DOES IT COME FROM?

There is a word so misunderstood that it has been applied to anything and everything in the world. Due to this abuse, many people have totally forgotten its true meaning. That word is *integrity*. It is a powerful word that should not be used carelessly.

Integrity by definition means an undivided state of being. The root of the word actually comes from the mathematical term *integer*, which means a complete entity. People use the word *integrity* to describe people whom they consider to be honest, loyal, and trustworthy. The problem with exclusively assigning these morals to the word *integrity* is that when someone is not honest, loyal, and trustworthy, we claim, "They have lost their integrity." Before long, we are let down by enough individuals that we start to wonder if there is any integrity left in the world at all.

Before we go any further, I want you to know that *honesty, loyalty,* and *trust* are priceless jewels that should be used to describe people of integrity. But they are only half of the equation. *Integrity* is a word used to describe the whole person, not just the good half. It describes the strengths as well as the shortcomings. A person of integrity is a person who is willing to be genuine and sincere, even if it means being vulnerable and exposing weaknesses.

The reason there is such a lack of integrity in the world today is because we expect someone else to have all the answers. We live in an imperfect world, and yet we are always in search of the perfect person—one who always knows what to do and is able to solve any problem.

Listen to the speeches politicians give when they run for office. Hear how they structure each line to appear as if they are in possession of the perfect solution. They use catchphrases and sound bites to create the sense of confidence that the public is longing for, and then once they find themselves elected and expected to perform, the reality of not having all the answers becomes a painful pill to swallow.

That's when the catchphrase on the "Vote for me" bumper sticker does not quite measure up to the expectation, and the disenfranchised public who voted for the candidates say they are not people of integrity. The ones who elected them to office are the first to point their finger and say that the newly elected officials are not doing what they promised.

> A person of integrity is a person who is willing to be genuine and sincere, even if it means being vulnerable and exposing weaknesses.

Believe me, had the candidate seeking office run by saying, "I really don't know how to solve the problems we are facing, because I am just a man like every other man. But if you elect me, I promise I will do my best, work hard, never quit, and try not to let you down," he might have run with integrity, but he would not have been elected—not even for dogcatcher. So, who is to blame—the man who said what you wanted to hear, or the people who wanted to hear it?

You will find that at every level of relationship, people have created masks and disguises to camouflage and hide their weaknesses. They show you only the strong side of the equation so that your confidence is built on what you see instead of all that's really there. When life's circumstances unmask the other half, you cry, "Foul!" That's why you commonly hear people say, "I have known them for years, and I would never have imagined they were capable of that!"

This type of behavior has impacted every relationship on the earth. It happens in every marriage. When two people are dating, they go to great lengths to create the appearance of complete perfection. They go so far as to pretend to like things that they really don't like, if it pleases the other party. They will endure what they find totally irritating if it will make them be *Mr.* or *Mrs. Right* in the sight of their suitors. I often laugh to myself when I hear a young man tell me, "Oh, pastor, she is perfect. She's the one for me. She loves NASCAR, college football, and video games—and she doesn't care how much I golf!" Wait until she hears you say, "I do." You'll get to watch cooking shows, parenting shows, and home etiquette shows while your golf clubs rust in the garage. What happened? What changed? The answer is nothing; you are simply having the opportunity to meet the other half of the person.

Men are just as guilty. They will work on their appearance for hours when they are dating. A man will carefully pick his shirt, cologne, and hairstyle to go sit in a dark movie theater where you can't see the other person anyway. He will go to great lengths to plan the perfect evening, carefully choose his words, be on his absolute best behavior, and display the kind of charm that would make Cinderella swoon. Then when he gets married, he'll walk through the door, look at his domestic damsel, and say something sweet like, "Where's my dinner?"

My father has said many times, "If love is a dream, marriage is the alarm clock." He told his five children over and over again, "Anyone can be wonderful for two hours on a Friday night—the real person is at home locked in a cage, waiting to be let out." Those may be lines laced with humor, but they are loaded with truth. Tragically and all too often there are much deeper issues hidden other than hygiene, appearance, and entertainment preferences that people try to shroud from their spouse.

Some suppress it for a few months, others for a period of years, but when the entire picture is finally revealed, there is a feeling of betrayal, and statements like "You've lost your integrity" will be spoken. The truth is, only when all the pieces of the puzzle are put together has the first moment of integrity really occurred.

The moment you are willing to be your *true self*—the good, the bad, and the flat-out ugly—is when you come to the real point of integrity. Integrity is one of the purest forms of trust. It happens when you are willing to be totally vulnerable and exposed and no longer hidden behind the lone-ranger mask, trying to play the mysterious hero who rides off into the sunset.

You have reached integrity when you are willing to say, "Here I am, warts and all. What you see before you is the complete me, the genuine article, the sincere version. It's not the Sunday morning version or the office version or the boardroom presentation version but the truth—the whole truth and nothing but the truth." That kind of integrity allows a truly meaningful relationship to emerge.

ARE YOU SINCERE?

To live your life with integrity is to live with sincerity. Sincerity is more than the closing line in a letter. *Sincerity* is made up of two Latin words. The first is *sin*, which means without. The next part of the word is *cere*, which translates "wax." Put them together, and the word literally is translated "without wax." The origin of the word comes from the days when hand-carved marble statues were the prized possession of the rich and famous.

When someone acquired one of these works of art, he wanted to know, "Is it sincere?" Is it without wax? A sculptor might begin a new work of art and continue sculpting it for two or three years. Sometimes during the sculpting process, he might discover a fracture or weakness in the stone, and a crack would emerge. Rather than destroy his work or waste all his effort, often a sculptor would grind up a few chips of marble and mix it with some melted wax, with which he would fill in the flaws.

This was considered to be a suitable fix as long as the statue stayed in a fairly cool and dark place. However, a few moments of exposure in the hot sun and the wax would melt, and the crack would be exposed. The most valuable statues were, of course, the ones without cracks, so people would set the statues in the warm light of the sun to prove to the world they were sincere...without wax.

Anything can appear perfect as long as the surroundings are dark enough, but expose it to the light, and soon the truth is revealed. The best relationships are sincere ones, the kind that hold up to the intense exposure of the outside elements of the world.

The thing I like about integrity is that I can be sincere, have flaws, and still be complete. I'm not perfect; nobody is. Integrity and sincerity are attributes that refuse to hide the truth but say, "This is who I am; will you accept me anyway?"

People of integrity are willing to lay down their masks. They are willing to expose their entire face and are not afraid to address the heat of reality.

The Word of God commands us to be people of integrity. We are instructed: "But let your 'Yes,' be 'Yes,' and your 'No,' 'No,' lest you fall into judgment" (James 5:12). Let your word be your bond. It may not be the word everyone wants to hear, but once you have spoken it, that settles it.

> The moment you are willing to be your
> *true self*—the good, the bad, and the
> flat-out ugly—is when you come to the
> real point of integrity.

We hear people say, "There's too much double-talk these days." Double-talk comes from being double minded. People who are double minded are plagued with the problem of doubt, and the worst kind of doubt is self-doubt. With every decision they make, they doubt if they have made the right one, and, therefore, they make two. For as long as possible, they stand on both sides of the issue. The moment the verdict is clear, they jump to the side that seems most correct and say, "I told you so."

Everything in life for them is gray. There is no black or white, right or wrong. Whichever way the wind blows, that's the way they're going. Just the moment you think you've patterned their behavior and can predict what they'll do next, they change direction and leave you stranded. You really can't blame them; after all, they don't even know what they will do next.

THE DANGER OF DOUBT

The New Testament writer James describes double-minded people this way: "But let him ask in faith, with no doubting, for he who doubts is like a wave of the sea driven and tossed by the wind. For let not that man suppose that he will receive anything from the Lord; he is a double-minded man, unstable in all his ways" (James 1:6–8). God Himself looks at people like this and says, "I am not going to provide you with any of My blessings." Why should He? They are so full of doubt that if He blessed them, they would doubt it came from Him and wind up giving credit to something cheap and insincere like fate or luck.

> People of integrity are willing to lay down their masks. They are willing to expose their entire face and are not afraid to address the heat of reality.

The solution to the problem is not that difficult, but it does require a lot of courage—the kind of courage that is not afraid to be who you really are, the unique individual that God in heaven created you to be. You may not be like the rest of the world, and you certainly may stick out in the crowd, but until you are willing to be yourself, you will never be a person of integrity.

When you are courageous enough to be a person of integrity, you can then begin to build truly open, honest, sincere, loyal, and trustworthy relationships with the people in your life. When people know the complete you, they are capable of developing realistic expectations of you, the kind that keep them from being let down and disappointed.

When the relationships in your personal life become sincere and full of integrity, they impact every other area of your life. Does that mean that your relationships are perfect and will not have their ups and downs? Of course not. What it does mean is that no matter how high or low, because your relationship is genuine, it will be strong enough to last.

Relationships like these build strong families. Families like these build strong churches. Churches like these build great communities. Communities like these impact the culture of the city. Finally, cities like these develop a great nation that influences the entire world. That kind of integrity begins with you.

You may not have all of the answers, and you may have some flaws, but in spite of your imperfections, if you are a man or woman of integrity, you will be true to the relationships that God has placed in your life and do what you can to help the quality of life for those around you, and that kind of dependable integrity has the power to change the world.

INTEGRITY CREATES STABILITY

Too many unchurched people claim that the modern church today is filled with hypocrites. That's really a fancy word for *play actor*, someone who pretends to be something he is not. Such a person does not exhibit integrity and sincerity, two attributes required to create stability.

> Integrity is powerful. If you have the
> courage to try it, it can change your life.

At Cornerstone, we have this response to the argument of hypocrisy: "Please come in; there's always room for one more." There are no perfect churches because there are no perfect people. Too often the world outside the church is so willing to point the finger because too many within the church are pretending to be something that they are not.

Think about it. If we were all perfect, why would we need to go to church, anyway? We would have it all figured out and not require the grace, mercy, healing, and love that can be found in the house of God. However, that is not the case.

Churches need to strive to be bastions of integrity where those who are flawed can come and find the sincere and genuine love of God. They need a secure and stable environment to grow spiritually without fear of shame or blame. A church that is filled with integrity is one that puts the Word of God above everything else. The Word of God is truth (John 17:17). When the church puts the Word first, its members are willing to crucify pride, ego, and personality for Christlikeness. The Word of God tells us, "God resists the proud, but gives grace to the humble" (1 Pet. 5:5).

A church filled with that kind of integrity will always be searching for more room to accommodate the newcomers. People are won to Christ when they can genuinely see what Jesus has done in your life and are persuaded that if He can change you, then He can change anybody.

Integrity is powerful. If you have the courage to try it, it can change your life. Integrity will change everything from your street to Wall Street, from the church house to the White House. If you are a person who is willing to be identified by your integrity, then no matter how shaken things may get, you will be rooted in the place of stability.

If a man hasn't discovered something that he will die for, he isn't fit to live.[1]

DR. MARTIN LUTHER KING JR.

8

Loyalty—the Quality
of Your Character

A Lesson I'll Never Forget

I met retired General Leroy Sisco in the fall of

2007. He came to the church to ask if I would

consider being a part of an evening honoring

the wounded soldiers of the war on terror

from the battlefronts of Iraq and Afghanistan.

General Sisco founded an organization dedi-

cated to helping these young men rebuild

their lives after the wounds of war had cost them to sacrifice so much. I was honored that he had asked me and was thrilled to participate.

As my wife and I entered the building, we were escorted to a room filled with others who were in some way connected to the evening. Our host informed us that the guests of honor would be arriving soon. A few moments later, a number of young men, all in the prime of life, entered the room where we were gathered. Some were in wheelchairs, others learning how to manage with brand-new canes or crutches, and for others, prosthetics occupied the places where arms and legs once were.

None of them had to say a word; their wounds told their stories. Each of these young men had paid a price for their loyalty to the cause of freedom. I was moved to tears in a sudden wave of emotion as I watched these fathers and husbands, not too different from me, light up the room and warm every heart with their smiles.

As I walked to the podium to give the invocation, there were a number of dignitaries in the room from the governor to social and civil leaders. None of them were as impressive to me that evening as those who had watered the tree of liberty with their own blood.

As the program continued, I had the opportunity

to personally thank each of these heroes for their service to our country. I was so humbled when they, in turn, thanked me. Their lives had been forever changed while defending my freedom, and they wanted to tell me how much they appreciated the fact that I had taken part in an evening honoring their sacrifice.

The price they paid went well beyond what I could imagine. Their lives were changed forever; every moment of every day was going to be lived with the memory and physical reminder of what war had done. Those who were fathers had forfeited the opportunity to be able to walk or run or play with their children as I would with mine. Sons who were missing limbs would not be able to embrace their fathers as I could my father. There were fiancés who were now unable to carry their brides across the threshold, as I had done with mine. Yet all of them wanted to thank me. It was more than I could bear. I am the one who owed them the thanks for serving their country and paying a high price for my freedom.

None of them were upset or hostile about the effects that war had on their life. Not one looked at me with contempt for not having worn the uniform or served my tour. All of them, to the last, remarked how they wouldn't change a thing. They would go right back into the fight if they could.

Where does this kind of character—such selfless

determination to serve others, regardless of whether or not they are appreciated—come from? Loyalty is the only source of such amazing strength.

Often we are willing to do things for recognition or reward, but no amount of recognition on the earth could make up for the price these men had paid. Yet their spirits were unwavering, their resolve bright, and their outlook hopeful. Why? It was because they served from a sense of loyalty.

They were loyal to a cause that was so much greater than any one individual—the cause of freedom. They were loyal to a people who were not always appreciative of them. They were loyal to a government that was divided in their support, just to gain a few more points in the popularity polls and an opportunity for reelection. They were loyal to the men who fought beside them and to those who had fought for the same cause before them. They were loyal to their word and the oath that they made when they raised their right hands and solemnly swore before God to defend this nation against all enemies, both foreign and domestic.

That night I learned a lesson I'll never forget. I learned a lesson in true loyalty—the kind of loyalty that will pay any price to prove itself, even if it means laying down your own life.

As a society, we have forgotten what loyalty is and where it comes from. We strive for independence, not to enjoy the freedom it affords us, but so that we don't have to depend on our fellow man for fear we may end up owing him something. The payback that comes from the modern helping hand has caused us to isolate ourselves from the rest of the world. There was a time, however, when loyalty seemed to be woven into the very character of this nation.

People were loyal to their neighbors and communities. They were willing to extend their hands and help each other when the occasion arose. I remember hearing my father and grandfather tell me how people would assist each other in harvesting their crops, building a barn, starting a church, or constructing a home. Now, unless you have four waivers signed by two witnesses who promise to hold us harmless, we won't even invite the neighborhood kids over to play. We fear they might skin a knee and we'll get sued. Why? Because we have forgotten how to be loyal.

The days are gone when we lived by a sacred code that said, "If you are there for me, I'll be there for you." Yet that is the kind of loyalty these young warriors displayed to me that night in downtown San Antonio. The more I thought about it, the clearer it became: these heroes had learned to depend on one another and to *be there* for each other. Their loyalty to one another is what made them an effective and powerful force in battle. It's what gave them confidence in the most uncertain hours of their life.

The reason they thanked me for my very small role that evening had nothing to do with what I said and everything to do with the fact that—at that moment, on that night, in some small way—I was there for them. That kind of loyalty creates the kind of shatterproof character the world needs.

WHERE DID IT GO?

Loyalty is a characteristic that needs to be revived in order for this country to survive the challenging days ahead. Our nation was birthed by loyalty. If you listen to the voices of our sacred past, you may hear the whisper of a patriot who slept in the freezing snow of Valley Forge so we could have the freedom to vote—yet some stay home on election day. There may be the sacred melody of "Taps," the hallowed song birthed during the struggle of the Civil War as a sad reminder of the devastation division brings— yet we remain divided as red states and blue states.

> True friends are there even when you don't deserve them. They stick close when others cut and run.

You may see the uniformed crosses and markers that line the seashore on beaches like Omaha and Normandy, or visit the cold gray marble memorials covered with names of individuals that remind us that freedom is not free. But still we take freedom for granted, as if it were an entitlement and not a privilege. In doing so, we have forgotten the price that liberty brings with it and seem to have lost our sense of loyalty to this land that has afforded such opportunity to so many.

Loyalty is what drove the heroes of the past—and present—to combat the hard issues head-on and not look back. Loyalty is what causes the selfless side of life to rise to the surface so others may benefit and be blessed. Loyalty is the characteristic that snatches moments of triumph from hours of adversity.

Loyalty overcomes every barrier and erases all injustice. Loyalty drives the spirit of men to accomplish what seems impossible for natural ability to do. Without loyalty, your life and future are as uncertain as the darting flight of a swallow, but a life grounded in loyalty stands upon an unshakable and enduring rock.

ARE YOU LOYAL?

Anyone can demonstrate aspects of fidelity when there is a reward involved, but loyalty gives no promise of reward. The Bible says, "A friend loves at all times" (Prov. 17:17). A *true* friend is *loyal*. True friends are there even when you don't deserve them. They stick close when others cut and run. Does that describe you? It should.

I get a kick out of watching people who are fair-weather fans of different sports teams. Everyone loves a champion! When one team hoists the trophy on championship night, its fan base surges by the next morning. But if that team begins the following season with losses, the once-adoring fans turn to hostile adversaries in search of someone else to love.

Many people apply the same inconsistency to other more important areas of their lives, but these inconsistencies carry deeper consequences than those of a fair-weather fan. When the slightest discomfort arises in a relationship, it may cause some to abandon ship and quit. This "fair-weather" nature has impacted the politics that govern our nation, influenced the communities where we live our daily lives, infiltrated the churches where we worship, and infected our marriages and families.

If there is a difficult issue to be addressed as a country, we avoid it. If there is a matter that needs to be settled in our city, we debate it. If there is a difference to overcome at church, we change our membership. If there is a problem at home, we don't accept responsibility—we point the finger in blame and start finding fault. Why?

It is because we have forgotten how to be loyal. We no longer know how to be dependable or how to trust others enough to depend on them. We fail to see that in spite of one another's shortcomings, we are here to make each other stronger and more complete—even if it means having to sacrifice to do so.

Only when you are willing to be loyal will you ever be a dependable source for others. Loyal people are there no matter what. I remember when the movie *Titanic* was a smash hit at the box office. There were a number of memorable scenes, but the one that stuck with me had nothing to do with the Hollywood romance and everything to do with loyalty. It was how the director depicted the stringed quartet who played on the deck while the mighty and majestic vessel sank.

Knowing that they were facing certain doom, these men didn't break and run. They didn't catch the first lifeboat leaving, or even seek out life jackets; they simply continued to do their jobs and play their song. Faithfully they stood side by side and filled the night with the sound of the sacred hymn "Nearer, My God, to Thee" as their fates were sealed. Was it easy? No, but it took loyalty.

Humans sometimes develop a fatalistic nature that decides there is really no use in trying, because in the end, we are doomed anyway. In the world we live in today, this kind of thinking is ever more prevalent and acceptable, but it is by no means new.

I remember an account from American history when the Connecticut House of Representatives had gathered in Hartford to take care of the business of government. The morning of May 19 was unseasonably cold, and by noon, no sun could be seen in a sky black as midnight. Sudden winds began to rattle the walls of the capitol building, hail battered the roof, and, with every clap of thunder, even men of faith fell on their knees, convinced the day of judgment and wrath had come.

As a wave of fear and trembling swept the floor of the state congress, a few of the elected officials stood and demanded the Speaker of the House immediately adjourn the session to allow each and every man to fall on their faces before God and make their peace with the Almighty before entering into eternity.

It was at this time the Speaker of the House, Colonel Davenport, an ordained minister, came to his feet, pounded the gavel, and silenced the House with these words: "The day of judgment is either approaching or it is not. If it is not, there is no cause for an adjournment; if it is, I choose to be found doing my duty. I wish therefore that candles may be brought."[2]

Colonel Davenport thought it better to be loyal to his purpose and to those in the community that he was appointed to serve than to allow severe circumstances to dictate his behavior.

> Only when you are willing to be loyal will you ever be a dependable source for others.

When my great-grandfather was a pastor in the early 1900s in Oklahoma, what is now known as *the tragic period of the Dust Bowl* hit the central farming region of the United States. Many began to say, "The Lord will be back before the end of the year. The world is coming to an end, and there is no need to plant crops or work and toil this year."

Those who were loyal to their responsibilities to provide for their families plowed their fields and planted their crops. Even though it wasn't much, their harvest fed them through the winter. Those in my great-grandfather's church who did not plant a thing almost starved to death. Why? Because they thought their current crisis and circumstance gave them an excuse not to be loyal to their responsibilities.

I am hopeful that you are starting to get the picture that loyalty is a serious, ongoing thing. Loyalty takes no vacations, and it must be lived out and demonstrated in the lives of each generation if they are going to overcome the challenges they face.

Are you loyal?

Look at what loyalty has cost those who have been faithful to God. There's Meshach, Shadrach, and Abed-nego who loyally stood by one another in the flames of the furnace. It would have been easy for one to turn on the others, knowing they were facing certain doom:

- "Hey, King, he made me do it."
- "I wanted to bow, but old Shadrach thought it would be funny if we stood up."
- "It's not my fault."
- "Why, I'll even bow to you right now and from now on forevermore if you just don't throw me in that fire with my friends."
- "I never really liked them anyway, and as they say, all good things must come to an end."

Instead, they stood by each other all the way into the flames. And when they got in the flames, God stood with them. Why? He did it because He honors loyalty. "He remains faithful" (2 Tim. 2:13). He is a loyal God.

Look at Silas, who was willing to sing with Paul in prison rather than deny him following their arrest. (See Acts 16.) There are countless other accounts of saints who faced the executioner's sword, the lions' den, and the chopping blocks, all for loyalty.

Are you loyal? When things become difficult, are you dependable? When standing up for your beliefs becomes a matter of great inconvenience, will you stand anyway?

Without loyalty, you will never know what it feels like to truly live. Loyalty separates the heroes from the cowards. Cowards quit; heroes are loyal to the very end.

What will it take to turn this country around? You can probably guess by now—it will take loyalty. It will require men and women who are willing to be loyal to what our Founding Fathers stood for: life, liberty, and the pursuit of happiness. When, as a people, we become more dedicated to the future of our freedom than to our personal comforts, then we will once again be a great nation, worthy of the title "land of the free."

> Loyalty takes no vacations, and it must be lived out and demonstrated in the lives of each generation.

What will it take to turn our cities around? Loyalty. Loyalty from city hall to the school board, from the PTA to the pulpit—it will take individuals who are more concerned with the well-being of their fellow citizens than they are of their own well-being.

Do you know what set the Christian community apart from the rest of the world in the first century? Loyalty! During the plague that swept the Roman world in A.D. 165–180, those who were infected were thrown out in the streets to die. However, the Christians brought the sick into their own homes, nursed them, and comforted them to the point that the heathens and pagans exclaimed, "How they love one another!"

When that kind of loyalty is extended into the streets of our cities—when that kind of sacrifice is a part of our everyday lives—the most difficult issues can easily be resolved, and a true sense of community can be reborn.

Our churches need a good old-fashioned dose of loyalty. We need pastors who are willing to be loyal to God's Word. We need lay leaders who are not afraid to stand for the truth no matter the cost. We need faithful members who are willing to walk in love and unity even when the world tries its utmost to divide us.

The churches of America are pursuing an endless list of popular messages, instead of remaining loyal to one true message. Preachers are trying to market motivation rather than speak the truth in love. Members would rather be entertained and comforted than inspired and challenged. What can change all that? What converts a congregation from a glorified country club into the light of the world? Loyalty.

Loyalty will make your home stable and secure in uncertain times. When you read the parable of the two builders, you find that Christ asserted, "And the rain descended, the floods came, and the winds blew and beat on that house" (Matt. 7:25). It was never a matter of *if*; it was a matter of *when*.

You don't have to look very far these days to find people who are facing tough times. Believers and nonbelievers alike are enduring the storms of life. But those who have a home built on loyalty to the Word of God and loyalty to one another can endure any and every challenge.

IT'S NOT THE WEATHER ON THE OUTSIDE; IT'S THE RESPONSE ON THE INSIDE

The difference is not the weather on the outside; it's how you endure the storm on the inside. Loyalty will bring you through the storm. There is a common phrase with which we are all familiar: "Are you worth your salt?" There was a time when men were paid in salt. The Latin word *salarium*, meaning pension, and the English word *salary* are both derived from the Latin root word for salt, which is *sal*. Both are based on a time when the accepted form of currency was salt.

The Bible talks of a *salt covenant*, whereby two men entered an agreement with an exchange of salt. Since salt was a necessary ingredient for daily food, it was an easy step to connect the exchange of salt as part of a covenant. Each man would remove salt from his own individual pouch and exchange it for salt from the other man's pouch as they recited the words of their covenant with each other.

The only way for this binding contract to be broken was for the exact granules of salt that had been exchanged to be retrieved from one another's pouch and returned to the man who gave them. It was a lasting agreement that was virtually impossible to break. If one of the men ever betrayed his word and commitment, then this statement was made: "That man is not worth his salt." In other words, he's not loyal to his word. He is not loyal to his fellow man. His behavior has betrayed his commitment.

From the beginning of time, the people of the world succeeded or failed based on their ability to be loyal. This truth has not changed. It is time, once again, for each of us to determine that we will be a people worth our salt. We will be loyal to our word even if it costs us, loyal to each other even if it means great sacrifice, loyal to our history and heritage and to those who have paid a great price to make us free, loyal to God in heaven, and loyal to our families.

———

Loyalty can indeed bring a revival of greatness into every area of our lives, but without it we—as a nation, a generation, and a people—will not survive.

———

Loyalty can indeed bring a revival of greatness into every area of our lives, but without it we—as a nation, a generation, and a people—will not survive. Loyalty is a characteristic by which you must desire to be known.

'When a man is at his wits' end, it is not a cowardly thing to pray; it is the only way he can get into touch with Reality.[1]

OSWALD CHAMBERS

9

Prayer—the Language of Power

The Day a Miracle Said, "I Do"

Growing up as a pastor's son, I have been to more than my fair share of weddings. Some of them were beautiful expressions of love and commitment, while others could not have been more hilarious and off the wall had they been choreographed. However, there is one particular wedding that I will always remember—it was a moment when a walking miracle repeated her vows.

Thirty-one years ago, a young man walked into my father's office and expressed interest in being the minister of music at Cornerstone Church. For some time, the church leaders had been praying for a music minister. Up to this point my father had been directing the choir, teaching Sunday school, preaching the sermons, and setting up and tearing down chairs. Needless to say, we needed help, and God in His faithfulness provided it the day John Hagee met Johnny Gross. To this day, he remains our minister of music and is one of the most gifted individuals I have ever had the privilege to meet.

Johnny and his wife, Lestra, have three children who grew up with my siblings and me at the church. As it is when your families work closely together, your relationships develop, and lifelong connections are made. So it was, and is, with the Hagee children and the Gross family. To this day we stay in touch and often reminisce about the old days in Sunday school, youth group, or some juvenile adventure we took somewhere.

One memory that I will always cherish when I think about the Gross family was the day their youngest daughter, Lizzy, was married. Not that this wedding distinguished itself with pomp and circumstance, or that it was an over-the-top display of fashion and design, but for the simple fact that there at the altar stood the most powerful and tangible testimony of prayer that I have ever seen.

In 1991, Lizzy was a normal, healthy, eleven-year-old little girl. She was full of life and was the light of her parents' lives. About this time, Lizzy began to complain of double vision and would tell her parents that she was seeing two things when she knew there was only one. In an effort to disprove her claim, Johnny, her father, held one finger in front of her face and asked how many there were, only to hear her say, "Two," and see her point to the two different places where she saw them.

Her mother decided it required further investigation, so she took Lizzy to the optometrist to get an analysis. The first visit resulted in mixed reviews. The optometrist determined she had one of three possible problems: a lazy eye that would correct itself over time; multiple sclerosis, which would need further medical attention; or ocular myasthenia, which is a fancy term for weakening of the muscle around the eye.

Not quite satisfied with what she had heard and still a bit concerned, Lizzy's mother took her to an ophthalmologist for a second opinion. The visit was much more defining and alarming. His immediate recommendation was that Lizzy be rushed over to the hospital for a CAT scan and MRI because it appeared that she had a mass behind her eye in her brain, and it was, indeed, more serious.

Shaken by the news, the Grosses moved quickly and wondered what would happen next as they awaited the test results. The worst occurred. The tests determined that there was an inoperable mass, and, in the words of her new oncologist, "Lizzy will soon die a gruesome and horrible death."

I was a young teenager at the time when the news of Lizzy's diagnosis began to circulate through the church, and I recall how sobering it was every time I heard it. I had been fairly immune to most of life's tragedies, but this one was hitting very close to home—a family we all knew very well, a little girl who was dearly loved, and a mother and father who were in desperate need of strength and hope. They had nowhere to turn but to the Father above.

My dad called for a fast to begin immediately and for people to pray for Lizzy's healing. We had someone praying at the church around the clock.

Lizzy's mother began to post Scripture on the walls of their home and proclamations declaring the promises of God that the family could meditate and dwell on day and night. In spite of the desperate and ongoing efforts, Lizzy began to experience symptoms that confirmed the doctors' diagnosis. The eye affected by the mass began to turn outward to the point it could not be seen. She experienced the massive headaches and a loss of balance the doctors warned of, and more tests confirmed that things were not improving. Still, the Gross family, Cornerstone Church, and countless others around the nation were crying out to God on Lizzy's behalf.

We reached the bottom a few weeks later. My father came home from work one day with a very concerned look on his face. When my mother asked him what was wrong, he told her, "The school told Johnny to come pick up Lizzy today. Her vision is such that she can no longer function in the classroom." He told her how Johnny had come to his office and wept, asking what he should do. My father did what he had always done—he wrapped his arms around the man and said yet another prayer. Then he gave Johnny this advice: "Go home, give your baby an aspirin, and treat her like everything is going to be all right!"

Days went by, and Lizzy started to show some improvement even though the doctors had specifically said there would be none. Her eye started to move back to the center, and she complained less of the headaches that had been ailing her so frequently just a few days earlier. A few days later, her parents returned to the doctor's office for another appointment—a place where they had yet to receive any good news. However, to the doctor's amazement, there was real evidence of improvement. Just to be sure of what was going on, he ordered another CAT scan and MRI.

On the day of the test, Johnny took a family friend and fellow church member to the appointment with him. The entire church was praying, and everyone wanted to know what the results were going to show. Johnny went into the room with Lizzy as the machine scanned her body, and Mike, the family friend, waited in another room where the doctors were reading the results.

Mike stood speechless as one doctor said to another, "It's not there! There should be a tumor right here! It was there when she was scanned the first time. Where did it go? Are you sure it's gone?"

It was instantly obvious that the miraculous healing power of God had touched that eleven-year-old girl's life, which is something I know those doctors do not study in medical school but God still does every day.

Ten years later, the chapel where people had prayed for her around the clock was filled with those who were there to hear her recite her wedding vows. Out of all of the weddings this preacher's kid has witnessed, this was the only one where I saw a miracle say, "I do." Prayer is by far the most powerful force on earth.

SUCCESS THROUGH STRUGGLE

No one ever promised that life would be trouble free. As a matter of fact, all great achievements are a combination of success and struggle. Life, indeed, is filled with a series of circumstances that require you to be a person of action and sacrifice in order to enjoy the best things in life. If you are going to be up to the challenge, there is a very important area of your life that needs to be monitored and brought under control: your speech.

What you say reveals what you are thinking. Your thoughts are a forecast of your future. Proverbs says, "For as he thinks in his heart, so is he" (Prov. 23:7).

Note the Bible states that you think with your heart. We usually assign thoughts to our minds and feelings to our hearts, but here the Word tells us that the *heart life* drives the *thought life.*

Make no mistake about it; your thoughts are the compass that sets the course of your life on a path to greatness or settles for simple mediocrity.

So, how do you generate great thoughts to start you on the proper path? Some self-help gurus would tell you to stare in the mirror in the morning and repeat a series of positive affirmations to put you in the right frame of mind for the day. My problem with this approach is that I cannot take myself seriously when I'm making absurd faces while brushing my teeth. It's difficult to create a dynamic mood for the day while foaming at the mouth that's filled with Colgate.

I do, however, agree with the gurus that you can talk your way into a great frame of mind. But I don't think you can do this by talking to yourself. You talk your way to success through a struggle by communicating with the source of unlimited power—and that is God. The way you talk to God is through prayer.

Prayer is the most powerful force on the face of the earth. It has conquered nations, saved lives, cured disease, liberated the imprisoned, and changed the course of history. Most people are confused and frustrated about prayer. Some feel it's a discipline of memorization and recitation. Others approach it as if they are talking to a genie in a lamp—three short wishes, and it will soon be over. The truth is that prayer should not be frustrating any more than it should be mundane and rehearsed, nor should it be an imaginary moment of make-believe. Prayer is a real, effective, and simple process of learning how to communicate with God.

Life, indeed, is filled with a series of circumstances that require you to be a person of action and sacrifice in order to enjoy the best things in life.

Once you understand the joy of engaging in a conversation with the Almighty, you will quickly realize that prayer is the language of power.

PRAYER IS A *DIALOGUE*, NOT A MONOLOGUE

Too many people use prayer like a drive-through window—they do all the talking, and God does all the listening. When they are through praying, they expect their order to be filled so they can get on their way. That's not prayer.

Prayer is not getting God in heaven to do your will here on Earth; prayer is getting you ready on Earth to do the will of God in heaven. Prayer is the lifeblood flow of your connection to the unending resources of the Father.

On many occasions, my grandmother has told her children and grandchildren this faithful truth: "Some prayer, some power; much prayer, much power." Nothing really good happens until you pray, because when you pray, you have the opportunity to hear what God has to say on the subject.

Like all dialogue, it takes time to learn how to communicate effectively. We've all heard the following phrase, which is shared between friends: "You didn't have to say a word. I heard you loud and clear."

That was certainly true growing up at the Hagee house. My father was a master at nonverbal communication with his family. His body language and expressions were an open book to his forthcoming response. He could walk with his five children into a roomful of people and control them with his eyes. Why? Because we knew all too well what he expected of us. When we were getting ready to cross the line, what may have seemed like a twitch of his brow or a shift of chin to the uninitiated was actually a three-point sermon and an altar call to those who truly knew him.

You can get to a point in your prayer life with your heavenly Father where you can understand very clearly what He is communicating while others don't hear Him at all. You see this truth in the life of Job.

Job learned many things as he struggled with so much loss and pain. One of the things he learned was this: "I have heard of You by the hearing of the ear, but now my eye sees You" (Job 42:5). At a time when those closest to Job couldn't understand what was happening in his life, Job got to know the Lord so well that he was able to see what God was doing when others could not.

How did this happen? He talked with the Lord. In Job 38 we read, "Then the LORD answered Job...and said...prepare yourself...I will question you, and you shall answer Me" (Job 38:1–3). God and Job had some intense conversations. In the midst of great struggle, Job achieved some great results. Not only did he receive twice as much in his old age as he had before his trial, but he also knew the Lord personally to the point that he could say, "I hear You loud and clear."

Job's experience is evidence that God wants to talk to you as much as you want to talk to Him. But it is only through practice that you will be able to hear what God has to say. Like all unfamiliar voices, you must learn to recognize His voice.

I have often had people challenge that truth by boasting, "Oh, believe me, I would know if *God* was talking *to me*." If that were really true, how do you explain that as a child, Samuel heard the voice of the Lord three times before he recognized who it was? The answer is that he was hearing a brand-new voice for the first time. However, once he became familiar with the sound of God's voice, he never forgot it. I suspect there are people who hear God's voice all the time; they just don't know it and cannot recognize it.

Prayer is not getting God in heaven
to do your will here on Earth; prayer is
getting you ready on Earth to do the
will of God in heaven.

When you approach prayer from the perspective of a dialogue where you can hear and receive instruction from God, great things are in store. For example, when you talk to me, you will receive a perspective that is subject to my opinion, based on my traditions, disposition, and the way I was raised.

However, when you talk to God, you will receive His divine instruction, which empowers you to succeed in every situation, no matter how big or small. My opinion—or for that matter, anyone else's—may cloud the issue and make it more difficult, but God's direction will cause the crooked way to be made straight, the impossible barriers to be opened, and will give the direction and insight that you need to achieve greatness and success in every area of life. The truth is, nothing exciting begins to happen until you have prayed.

HOW DO I TALK WITH *GOD*?

Now that you have a proper perspective on prayer, there are some things I recommend you do when you pray. Some people make excuses about why they don't pray. Maybe you've heard some of these:

- "Well, I just don't know what to say."
- "I get so distracted."

And my personal favorite...

- "When I pray, I get it all said in a few minutes...and then I'm done."

Don't get me wrong; I am not an advocate of rehearsed, prescribed amounts of prayer, but I do believe that you should approach your conversation with God with the same amount of courtesy that you would anyone else.

For example, if you were going to talk to one of your closest friends, would you only talk about yourself? Of course not—you would want to know about that person because you truly care for him or her. The same should be true about your conversation with God. You don't need to spend all of your time talking about yourself. I recommend you spend your time talking about who the Lord is and what He has done in your life. One of the reasons people find it difficult to develop an extended prayer life is because they focus on a very limited subject—themselves. If you want a limitless prayer life, discuss an unlimited topic—God.

I am truly blessed with a beautiful wife and two wonderful

children. From time to time, someone will pay them a compliment. When they do, I don't bashfully blush and say, "Thank you." I wholeheartedly agree with them. As a matter of fact, I start telling them stories to support the fact that my wife and kids are just as wonderful as they believe them to be. I don't do this from a sense of ego or because I like to brag; I do it because I love them so much I can't help myself! I'll talk about them every time the opportunity allows.

The same should be true regarding your relationship with God in prayer. You should be able to talk about Him for hours. When you consider all that He has done for you, you ought to be able to go on and on. David said in Psalm 143:5, "I remember the days of old; I meditate on all Your works. I muse on the work of Your hands." It's not bragging; *it's love.* If you want to develop a truly great prayer life, talk less about yourself and more about Him. You can get lost for hours thinking about all He has done for you.

The truth is, nothing exciting begins to happen until you have prayed.

Once you've spent some time talking about who God is, then you can start talking about all that He has done. Have you ever sat around the table with family and friends and shared stories with each other? "Do you remember the time...?" and "Oh, how about when...?" Taking those walks down memory lane help you keep in mind how valuable your relationships with your loved ones have been, what you've helped each other through, and how you've stood by one another through thick and thin.

If you will apply these same truths to your conversations with God, you will experience some of the most meaningful and powerful moments you'll ever spend with Him. When you say, "Father, I thank You…" and begin filling in the blank with all God has done, then you will soon realize that the challenges you face today are no match for the God who has done so much for you already.

After these two topics have been covered, your prayer can then turn to another great topic—the needs of others. This is called *intercession*. It is when you make your presence known to God concerning a matter that may not involve you at all. When you take the time to pray for others, God finds the time to bless you.

If you want a limitless prayer life, discuss an unlimited topic—God.

For example, read these two particular passages from Scripture. Psalm 122:6 says, "Pray for the peace of Jerusalem: 'May they prosper who love you.'" This psalm gives instruction to intercede for a particular place: the City of God, the Holy City of Jerusalem. Notice that this command comes with a blessing: "May they prosper who love you." The text shows very clearly that when you pray and intercede for this particular place, the blessing of prosperity is yours.

You may ask, "How does that work?"

To be perfectly honest, I am not nearly as concerned with the *how* as I am convinced that it works. I have seen it work over and over again in the lives of those who faithfully put it to use.

This past year we were blessed to celebrate my father's fiftieth anniversary in full-time ministry. Over the course of the weekend, he was honored for many achievements. On Sunday morning he shared his thoughts and reflections with his congregation in a very meaningful and heartfelt sermon. He thanked members of our church who had faithfully served over the years. He spoke of the favor of God that had been on his life and ministry and the fact that he was not through yet. Then he shared with us one of the many secrets to his success. He said, "I believe that God has been faithful to me because I have always supported the nation of Israel."

When he said that, immediately Psalm 122:6 came to mind. I can attest to the truth of this verse from observing my father's life and the lives of others who have put it to practice.

Another scripture that illustrates intercession is found in 1 Timothy 2:1–2, we are instructed to make "supplications, prayers, intercessions, and giving of thanks" for all men. The list begins with kings and is expanded to all who are in authority, with a promise of this blessing: "...that we may lead a quiet and peaceable life."

Think about what a profound impact there would be on your life if you took the time to pray that God would bless the lives of every individual in a place of authority in your life. It would include all those in every level of government, including the president, the mayor, your city council representative, your children's schoolteachers and administrators, your pastor, and your boss at work. All these people need your prayers. They all make decisions that impact your life. You can avoid some of life's difficulties if you will be faithful to intercede on their behalf.

> When you take the time to pray for
> others, God finds the time to bless you.

The list of those for whom you pray can be as deep and wide as you would care to make it. This is the point: As you add more and more names to the list, you begin to realize there are a lot of people who can truly be a benefit to *your life* if you will only take the time to intercede for them through prayer.

The more you talk to God, the more success you will experience in every area of your life. The more success you experience, the more you will realize that prayer is the most powerful language on the face of the earth.

*Worship is our declaration of dependence
and pledge of allegiance to the Lamb.*

MATTHEW HAGEE

10

BE LIBERATED BY YOUR WORSHIP

A Melodic Truce

Twice in the twentieth century, the world has been

engulfed in war. The struggle for power and control

shook the greatest nations on the face of the earth

as her sons sacrificed themselves on battlegrounds

that are spoken of in hushed and revered tones as

we remember the brave. Personally, I have always

loved history and enjoyed reading the smallest

details surrounding major events in order to try to discover some buried treasure from days gone by.

There is one such account from the dreaded days of World War I. The misery of trench warfare had weighed heavily on both the Allied forces and their German adversaries, and very little was being accomplished in the deadly battles that sent thousands to their doom. This certainly doesn't seem the proper setting for such an account, but from the battlefield of Belleau Wood comes a war story you will never forget.

Christmas was approaching, and both sides of the battlefield were exhausted and tired of fighting. As the darkness of night loomed overhead and men hunkered beneath their protective mounds, a faint sound broke the silence of the night.

A German solider began to quietly sing a melody that reminded all those who heard it of another world far away from the hell of the war that they faced. It was a song that spoke of a quiet night outside the city of Bethlehem in the hills of Judea, where angels watched a virgin give birth.

As he continued singing the well-known hymn, he was suddenly joined in the song—except not from his comrades sitting next to him. It was the voice of one of his enemies on the opposing side. Before long, another solider joined the tune, and then another, until a chorus of commandos' voices filled the air on that night no longer divided by ideals, combat, and orders but united in the heavenly peace.

That Christmas morning, the German soldiers and British soldiers met in the middle of the battlefield for a spontaneous armistice agreed upon not after intense hours of negotiation brought on by terms from diplomats, but after a song of worship about the Prince of Peace sung from the hearts of those who were searching for what only His presence can provide.[1]

Even in the horror of war, praise will liberate and comfort you like nothing else will.

WORSHIP IS A PRAYER SET TO MUSIC

There is a very natural progression from the topic of prayer to the subject of worship. Prayer is more about who God is and what God has done and less about you, and the more you focus on Him when you pray, the deeper and more meaningful your prayer life will become. Worship is very simply the thoughts of your prayer life put to music.

Did you know that God is a music lover? Music is so near to His heart that in heaven, at this very moment, a choir of angels is singing praises to Him as He sits on the throne. Not only does He truly enjoy the music of heaven, but He also goes out of His way to be involved in our worship here on Earth. Psalms tells us that the Lord inhabits the praises of His people.

When He hears His children on Earth singing songs about Him, He literally leaves His throne room and shows up in your room. The scripture describes it this way: "But You are holy, enthroned in the praises of Israel" (Ps. 22:3). When you worship the Lord, you build a royal chamber for Him to abide in, and the greatest benefit of this particular throne room is that you get to abide there too.

Worship is not just the opening portion of a church service or something that is reserved for a certain time and place. Worship is appropriate at any time and in any place. Worship is the song that can set you free. It is the only music that will escort the presence of God Himself into your situation. And when you can sing a song that will make God show up, that, my friend, is a great song. That is a rock-solid and unshakable melody.

PERSONAL, POWERFUL, NOT OPTIONAL

There are a few things you need to know about worship. First, *worship is personal*. Many people find this difficult to understand because of their context for worship. Most people view worship in relationship to the modern church services available to us every Sunday. They understand worship to be singing songs that are led by an individual who is accompanied by musicians and often a group of singers or a full choir. Due to the major production efforts that people see involved in worship today, many feel worship is not possible unless there is someone to lead them and an orchestra to back them up. This is just not so.

Whether you realize it or not, every time you become involved in the act of worship, you do so because you made a choice as an individual to praise the Lord. No one forced you into it; you personally decided to participate. The worship leader, musicians, singers, and atmosphere may have encouraged you, *but they didn't force you.*

I see this firsthand almost every Sunday when I lead worship at Cornerstone Church. There are thousands of people in every service, and, indeed, most participate enthusiastically. But there is always one or two who stand there with their arms folded and with a look on their face that says, "I'm not gonna, and you can't make me!" They are exactly right; they cannot be forced into worship. It is not a group activity; worship is a personal choice. You either choose to do it, or you choose not to do it.

At times the topic of worship in the Bible is referred to as the *sacrifice of praise.* The nature of a sacrifice is personal—your sacrifice doesn't cover me, and my sacrifice doesn't cover you. We each choose to sacrifice as individuals in order for the blessings of God to become a reality in our lives. This was as true in the days of the Old Testament as it is today.

Worship is not just the opening portion
of a church service or something that
is reserved for a certain time and place.
Worship is appropriate at any time and
in any place.

In the Old Testament, many people may have participated in the same service under the leadership of the same priest, but they were there as individuals to offer their sacrifice unto the Lord. If you brought your lamb to be laid upon the altar, someone else could not claim any part of it. It was yours, and yours alone. If another person was going to offer anything to the Lord, he had better bring his own lamb, because there was no such thing as community property. The sacrifice was required, and it had to be personal in order to count.

It's the same with a sacrifice of praise. We may be in the same service under the leadership of the same pastor, but if I am going to receive a blessing from God, I have to offer my heart in worship to Him. And if you are going to receive a blessing, you had better do the same for yourself.

Now, keep in mind that God requires the sacrifice. I have often had discussions with people who are adamant that they will not be instructed or told how to worship. I have told many of them that I am not the one that they are worshiping, so arguing with me is a waste of time. You don't owe me an explanation, because your praise is not about the observation of any man-made rule on Earth—it is about the perspective of God in heaven.

People who find it difficult to worship God are generally immature spiritually. They are like my son when he sits down at the dinner table. There are children who eat to live and others who live to eat. My son, John William, by his birthright, falls into the latter category.

At the age of two, he does not sit at the table and shower his parents with praise and thanksgiving because of the meal they have prepared and provided. Rather, like a thirty-two-inch tornado, he tears through his plate as if he were being judged in a timed event. Occasionally there will be commands for more or a pointed finger and a squeal if there's something he seems to want or need. And then he gets to a point where he pulls off his bib and declares, "I'm done!"

No thought of a thank-you or "Can I help clean up?" or even a conversation about "How was your day?" Why? It is because at his age, he is too young to comprehend the source of his blessings.

As he grows and matures, different standards will be expected for his table manners—including one that reflects more appreciation of what has gone into providing this meal. However, at the age of two, I'm willing to be patient and wait on him to mature. To be perfectly honest, I even think it's kind of cute. But when he gets to be twenty-two, all of that had better change.

It is not my intent to remind you what it is like to eat with a toddler but to say there are some of God's children who treat Him in much the same way. They are too immature to take the time to comprehend where their blessings come from, and in their immaturity, they never slow down long enough to say thank you. They do not take the opportunity to worship the Lord for what He has done. This shouldn't be!

The Bible tells us that the Lord is patient; as a matter of fact, in Romans 15:5, Paul calls Him "the God of patience." But there comes a point in everyone's life when God requires you to mature and recognize who He is and to give Him the praise He deserves.

God is your provider, protector, and the source of everything good and perfect in your life. To refuse to worship Him is unacceptable. He deserves glory when the sun comes up and praise when the moon shines at night. Without Him, your next breath would not be possible. Because of Him, everything you have has been made possible. So, believe me, He deserves your personal sacrifice of praise and your song of worship.

Not only is worship a personal choice, but it is also *a powerful choice*. Throughout the pages of God's Word, you can find example after example of when worship played a critical role in a major victory.

Look at 2 Chronicles 20. King Jehoshaphat is outnumbered and overwhelmed. A number of armies are marching against him, and their purpose is his total annihilation. Jehoshaphat, in an effort to be a great king and make a great decision, gets in connection through prayer with his source of greatness—God in heaven.

People who find it difficult to worship
God are generally immature spiritually.

Through this moment of dialogue, God tells the king, "Do not be afraid nor dismayed because of this great multitude, for the battle is not yours, but God's" (2 Chron. 20:15). As you read further down in the chapter, you discover that Jehoshaphat appointed people to sing to the Lord and march in front of his army. The song was not that long, but it packed plenty of punch: "Praise the LORD, for His mercy endures forever" (v. 21).

With that one phrase of worship, God set one ambush after

another for the enemies of Israel until, Scripture reports, "no one had escaped" (v. 24). Worship had brought a total victory. That's powerful.

Before we leave this example, I think it is important to take into account all of the portions of this equation that brought about such great results. First, Jehoshaphat, king of Israel, was faced with a serious problem. Rather than just reacting, "Jehoshaphat...set himself to seek the LORD" (v. 3). The Hagee translation says that he was not going to get off of his knees until he had his answer. I like the fact that when he needed an answer to bring stability to his trembling life, he looked to the source where stability could truly be found—God Himself. What a truly great leader.

Once the king received the response, he acted upon it. The prophet Jahaziel told the king, "The battle is not yours, but God's" (v. 15). Jehoshaphat responded by doing the one thing he knew he could do to bring the presence of God to Earth—worship. Remember, the Lord "inhabitest the praises of Israel" (Ps. 22:3, KJV).

It makes perfect sense—if this is God's fight, then get out of the way and let Him fight it. Through his willingness to place his confidence in God, not only was Jehoshaphat victorious over those who attacked him, but also it took three days to carry home the spoils of war (2 Chron. 20:25). That is what you call *a real victory.*

I like how the story ends. They threw a two-day concert in honor of God, who had given them the victory. On day one, they assembled in the valley where the battle took place, and Scripture reads, "There they blessed the LORD" (v. 26). Then, with

Jehoshaphat out in front, they returned to Jerusalem carrying stringed instruments and trumpets to the house of the Lord to continue celebrating what God had done. Not only did they receive the victory, but they also were liberated from those who were trying to oppress them, they increased in their material resources for their obedience unto God, and they set an example for the others to follow who find themselves overwhelmed by circumstances that seem to be out of control.

Not only had worship brought them the victory in battle, but it was also the final by-product of the fight. Psalm 34:1 says, "I will bless the LORD at all times"—before, during, and after the battle is over.

Now, more than ever, many people are facing a multitude of problems, just as Jehoshaphat did. If worship worked for him, it will work for you. No matter the circumstances you find yourself in, regardless of the issues that are stacked against you, the power of worship will bring you through.

Worship will not only bring you a victory, but it will also set you free. Look at the case concerning the apostle Paul and his ministry partner Silas. They had found themselves locked inside the darkest cell of a Roman prison—beaten, shackled, and chained. This is not the exact moment you would think they would be in the mood for a song; however, Acts 16:25, states, "At midnight Paul and Silas were praying and singing hymns to God, and the prisoners were listening to them." They had not allowed the drastic and devastating events of the day to change their attitudes concerning who God was and what He had done for them.

> God is your provider, protector, and the source of everything good and perfect in your life. To refuse to worship Him is unacceptable. He deserves glory when the sun comes up and praise when the moon shines at night.

The result? The earth began to shake and the foundations of the prison began to rumble as two of God's children went from captivity to freedom. I promise you, worship is powerful. Worship will defeat your enemies, bring you total victory, and liberate you from all forms of restriction.

There are still some who hear testimonies like this and think, "Well, I just don't feel like it." Worship is not a matter of feeling; *it is a matter of fact.* You either choose to worship or you choose not to worship. Worship has nothing to do with feeling. Your circumstances here on Earth may change from one moment to the next, but nothing in heaven changes.

The same God that you worshiped when you felt like praising and when everything was going right is still on His throne right now, and He is still worthy of your praise, whether you feel like it or not. All too often we allow our surrounding circumstances to dictate our behavior rather than allowing the proper behavior to dictate our circumstances.

If you are going to enjoy success in spite of the struggle, then you are going to have to choose to make worship a part of your everyday life. Worship is personal and powerful, but *it is not optional.*

The Bible says, "Let everything that has breath praise the Lord" (Ps. 150:6). As long as you are inhaling and exhaling, you are expected to worship. I like the way Psalm 115:17 puts it: "The dead do not praise the Lord." The point is that if you find it difficult to worship the Lord, you need to check your pulse. You may be physically alive, but you are spiritually flatlined.

One of the reasons worship is so powerful is due to the fact that it reminds your enemies that you are still alive and kicking. It is a testament that in spite of their attempt to silence you, you still have a song to sing. Rather than discourage you, they have done nothing more than give you one more reason to rejoice.

If your life feels like a war zone, a song of worship can create a sudden sense of peace. If you are in search of direction for the uncertain path that lies ahead, the power of praise can lead you to victory. There are times when worship will change the situation and trial that you are facing, and then there are times when it may not alter your scenario one bit, but it will change your perspective and enable you to see the situation in a entirely different light.

The psalmist asked this question:

> Why are you cast down, O my soul?
> And why are you disquieted within me?
> Hope in God, for I shall yet praise Him
> For the help of His countenance.
>
> —Psalm 42:5

Without a doubt, the writer of Psalm 42 was experiencing a series of unsettling circumstances that caused him difficulty. His words express the heavy emotional burden that is weighing down his soul to the point that it has been disquieted or, in modern English, disturbed. I'll even go one step further and say that the author of this psalm was starting to complain.

Isn't that our natural tendency when we are spiritually disturbed? We begin to list all of the things that are not going as we wish they would, and we start filling the air with how we deserve so much better. I like the way the verse captures the inner struggle by asking these questions: "Self, why are you acting this way? What is the value in your long list of complaints? We've been here before, and every time we've been in this spot, we have put our hope in God and begun to sing Him a song of praise."

The psalmist gives himself some good counsel by saying, "Hope in God" (v. 5).

Look at the result of the change in the behavior: "I shall yet praise Him for the help of His countenance." *Countenance* is an old English word for *face*. The picture we see in this verse is of the face of God turning in the direction of the one who is singing His praise. It is as if out of all the sounds that fill the heavens, there is one that causes everything to stop and God to pay attention.

Worship is not a matter of feeling;
it is a matter of fact.

One of the names for God in the Bible is *Jehovah-Jireh*, directly translated "the God who sees." Abraham called the Lord *Jehovah-Jireh* on the day that God provided the ram from the thicket for the sacrifice in the place of his son Isaac. When Abraham had a real need, the God who could see the need could also provide the answer. This is where the word *provision* comes from. When you break the word down, you notice that vision is its root. The message is that before you can meet the need, you have to see the need.

How does this apply to the topic of praise and to the Psalms? When you praise the Lord for the help of His countenance and He turns His face in your direction, He suddenly can see all that is going on in your life, and He begins to supernaturally meet your need.

Think of it in these terms: when you are in real need and looking for real answers, you can fill the air with complaints and, at the end of your rant, be out of breath and still in trouble, or you can fill the air with a song of praise and receive the full attention of the Lord God, who can really do something about the problem that you face.

The more you understand the power of praise, the more it will continually be in your mouth.

I will greatly rejoice in the Lord,
My soul shall be joyful in my God;
For He has clothed me with the garments of salvation,
He has covered me with the robe of righteousness.

ISAIAH 61:10

11

Joy—the Choice of Greatness

The Power to Choose

The flight from Tel Aviv to New York is never
short, and this one promised to be especially
long. There, crammed in the middle of the aisle
back in the coach section sat my mother and
father, waiting to endure their journey home
and reunite with their children after a tiring trip.

My mother has never been the best of fliers, and she was not looking forward to this particular flight. As she tried repeatedly to get comfortable, as if that's even possible for eleven hours in the air, the man next to her tried to engage her in conversation.

"Hello, my name is Sol; what's yours?"

"Are you going to eat that?"

"Do you mind if I turn on my light and do some reading?"

Finally, after my mother gave my father one glaring glance too many, they switched seats so Mom could rest and Dad could get to know the man sitting beside her. Sol asked my mother if he could have the yogurt that her airsickness was keeping her from eating, and as he reached to take it, his extended arm revealed a tattoo that the Nazis had placed there years before.

This man's story would change my father's perspective forever. For the next eleven hours, Sol Weinglas shared with my father his personal account of his childhood in some of the most unspeakable circumstances you could imagine. When Sol was a young boy in Poland, he was one of eight children in the Weinglas house. By the time he was a young man following World War II, only he and one brother had survived.

Sol spared no words when he described how

the Nazis immediately began to use food as a weapon when they took power in Poland. If you were going to eat, you had to get your rations from them. Once they checked your papers, they could identify whether you were Jewish or not. From there, they isolated the Jews into neighborhoods that became known as the ghettos.

On the night that the Jews were rounded up and thrown into an isolated neighborhood, people who had slept in king-sized beds with satin sheets the night before suddenly found themselves lying on a strange floor surrounded by strange people, hoping that tomorrow would somehow be better than the horror of today. In a world that was changing moment by moment and spinning out of control, the priorities of life changed instantly.

No longer did family wealth matter; now the focus was simply surviving as a family. The shock of it all cost many, mostly the elderly, their lives. They could not bear the instantaneous reversal and brutal world in which they found themselves. When one passed away, the Nazis required that they be laid in the street, and from there they would be carted off and disposed of.

The conditions in the ghetto made each and every meal precious. People would do anything for food. Sol described how he would sit with others as they all described the best meal they had ever eaten. They imagined where they would eat that night in their dreams, and what would be served at the make-believe meal in the theater of their mind.

Some took hunger to such a level that they ate grass in an effort to keep from starving, only to have the blades of grass punch holes in their stomachs and cause them to become sick and die. As the war raged, the Nazis grew more desperate. Finally they came to Sol's ghetto, rounded up every family, placed them on a train, and sent them to a place known as Aushwitz.

When the train stopped, after hours of standing shoulder to shoulder without food, water, or sanitation, they were offloaded from the cars and divided into two lines. There a man in a white coat, later known to the world as Dr. Josef Mengele, would evaluate those who were strong enough to work and those who were not.[1] Once the Jewish prisoners understood what was happening, women tried pricking their fingers and pinching their cheeks in an attempt to create any sign of color and health to convince this monster in a medical coat that they had the strength to live. It was in this line that Sol saw his mother, father, and all but one of his siblings for the last time.

Sol went from one hardship to another. He

continued his story by telling my father about his liberation from the death camp and his service fighting in the war for Israel's independence. He was in the streets of Tel Aviv on the morning a nation was born. While living in Israel, he entered a school to learn the art of diamond cutting and the business of the diamond trade.

Later in life, he moved to New York and opened a very successful jewelry store in the middle of Manhattan on Forty-seventh Street. Every day from that first meeting until the day he died, he was always filled with joy and had a smile on his face whenever my father saw him or talked with him.

My father was finally persuaded to ask him, "Sol, for all that you have been through, why are you not at all bitter?"

His answer was powerful and some of the soundest advice I have ever heard. He told my father, "In spite of the freedoms and liberties that I lost as a child, and with everything the horror of the Holocaust took from me, the one thing that was mine, and mine alone, every minute of every hour of every day, was the freedom to choose my attitude. The Nazis could do to me physically whatever they pleased, but they could not tell me how to respond emotionally. And in spite of the nightmare I lived through, I chose to live through it with the attitude of joy."

Because he chose to be joyful, Sol Weinglas lived his life filled with a miraculous and genuine compassion for others and a love for humanity when he had every reason and excuse to behave otherwise. Whether good or bad, he would always say, "You never lose your ability to choose your attitude."

Sol was a joyful man to his final day.

LET JOY BEAR THE BURDEN

The world we live in is indeed a formidable place. There is an endless list of issues and situations that can weigh us down to the point that it may indeed seem impossible to be happy. As a matter of fact, experts say, "An estimated 26.2 percent of Americans ages 18 and older—about one in four adults—suffer from a diagnosable mental disorder in a given year."[2] That is no small number.

Doubt, depression, discouragement, and despair are the four Ds that seem to impact and affect our everyday lives. While people see good things happening in the world, many doubt that anything good will ever happen to them. The tinted lens of depression seems to cloud everyone's picture of life. In spite of all the wonderful things we have to enjoy, many are discouraged over what they don't have, and even fewer feel they have the ability to change any of it, so they live in relative despair.

Why all this gloom? Because we choose to be depressed and discouraged.

Joy is a choice you make. It is not brought on by circumstance or created by opportunity. Joy is the result of the decision you make on a daily basis, and it totally impacts your life. It is your attitude that makes you joyful.

I have seen people who have all of the pleasures life can afford. They are healthy, they have wealth and resources and plenty of family and friends, and yet they are as miserable as the hound dog on *Hee Haw*. Then there are those who are experiencing much more desperate circumstances yet are as happy and content as a life can be. Why? Joy is not a by-product of an environment; joy is something you choose or refuse. The fact is, it's up to you.

There are a number of things that you can choose to be happy about. You can be joyful about your purpose in life. The apostle Paul wrote that he would finish his race with joy (Acts 20:24). He knew his purpose was to share the gospel and spread the news of Christ and His Holy Spirit, and he was determined to do it with a joyful heart.

It was this kind of determination that enabled him to endure all of the hardship life threw his way. Paul knew more about peril and pestilence than ten men combined, yet, he said, "For I consider that the sufferings of this present time are not worthy to be compared with the glory which shall be revealed" (Rom. 8:18).

Paul's point was this: There is a better day coming. You may certainly have to endure heartache and setback today, but keep your eye on the promise of tomorrow. What Paul endured would be enough to make ten others quit, but with joy in his heart he pressed on and pursued his purpose with a passion and joy.

Just as God had a purpose for Paul, He also has a purpose for you. He is sovereign and all knowing, and He, indeed, has a divine plan for your life. The greatest tragedy in life is not to die but *to live without knowing your purpose.* Purpose is what provides you with a sense of satisfaction. Solomon wrote in Ecclesiastes 6:3–6 that "a stillborn child" is better than the man who lives a dissatisfied life. Satisfaction comes from accomplishment, and accomplishment is the by-product of purpose.

In Colossians 1:16 we are told that all things were created and given purpose by God. There is no real mystery to doing the will of God and to knowing your purpose. Too often people will try to make that more difficult than it needs to be. The will of God begins with His written Word. When you are doing what His written Word requires of you, then the remainder of your purpose seems to fall into place.

> Joy is not a by-product of an environment; joy is something you choose or refuse.

So, where should you begin to look regarding what God requires of you? I like the words that Christ spoke when He said, "You shall love the LORD your God with all your heart, with all your soul, with all your strength, and with all your mind, and your neighbor as yourself" (Luke 10:27).

If you can fulfill that command—to put God above all else and others above yourself—then you will find the joy of God's purpose for your life. Once you begin to fulfill His purpose, the burdensome areas of life suddenly seem to become lighter. The challenges will not disappear; they simply become much more bearable because no longer are they combined with the confusion of why you are here and what God in heaven wants you to accomplish. The challenges then become opportunities for you to flourish in, because you have the joy and satisfaction of purpose to see you through.

The Real Power of Joy

Once you begin to know the joy of God's purpose for your life, you suddenly see that His purpose is also filled with His power. Look at the life of Elijah. God had a specific purpose for this prophet, and every time God told Elijah to move, he would arrive where the Lord sent him to find God's power waiting for him there.

When God sent him to the Brook Cherith, the power of God supernaturally fed him from the ravens that brought him room service (1 Kings 17:1–7). When he was sent to the widow's house, the power of God met him there (1 Kings 17:8–24). When he marched up Mount Carmel, God rained fire over his sacrifice (1 Kings 18:20–40). The power of God never fails to show up and fulfill His purposes in the lives of His children.

Jesus Christ gave His disciples a purpose: "Go into all the world and preach the gospel to every creature" (Mark 16:15). Then He sent them to a specific place and gave them power. "But you shall receive power when the Holy Spirit has come upon you" (Acts 1:8). God indeed has a specific purpose for your life, and He wants to fill you with the power to live it out. The first step is to joyfully choose to do His will.

Joy is not only a choice that can be found in your purpose, but it can also be a choice that is found in righteousness. One of the reasons we are a miserable people is because we make miserable choices. Life is a product of choice. When you make righteous choices, you reap righteous rewards that lead to joy.

Look at the infamous prodigal son. He made a series of unrighteous choices that removed the joy from his life. The farther away he walked from his father's house, the more miserable he became. The day he chose to return to his father's house is the day the joy showed up in his life again. Living a right life brought the joy back.

There are many people who are living depressed lives because of the poor choices they've made. Their confused sense of free will and independence has made them prisoners in a life they hate, but joy can set them free if they are willing to make choices based on God's commands.

THE JOY OF RESPONSIBILITY

Joy is found in responsibility. It is found in knowing you are needed by others who are counting on you. Recently, my wife and I decided it was time for our four-year-old daughter, Hannah, to take on the responsibility of feeding our Labrador. This is a chore that has long since lost its joy for me. I look at it as one more thing on my checklist to do in a day. But when we showed our little girl where the food was and how to fill the bowl and change the water, you would have thought we made her queen for the day. She gets up in the morning looking forward to feeding the dog. When I come home in the evening, she wants to know if she can feed the dog right then. As a matter of fact, our dog needs to go on a diet because my daughter enjoys her job so much.

If you can fulfill that command—to put God above all else and others above yourself—then you will find the joy of God's purpose for your life.

God engineered us to enjoy responsibility. Look at the life of Jacob recorded in the Old Testament. He spent most of his life frustrated, terrified, and running. He stole his brother's birthright and ran to Uncle Laban's house. He wanted to marry Rachel, Laban's daughter, but instead he was tricked into marrying Leah, her sister. (See Genesis 29.) One week later Jacob was given Rachel as well, but he never confronted his deceitful uncle about the "bait and switch." Instead, he chose to spend the next seven years frustrated, working to pay Laban for the woman he loved.

Then his uncle cheated him out of his wages. Again, rather than confront him, Jacob ran.

However, now he has a different problem. He's terrified because he's running right back to his brother, Esau.

Jacob didn't find real happiness until God confronted him in an all-night wrestling match and "touched" his hip (Gen. 32:22–30). The next morning Jacob couldn't run anymore; in fact, he had a limp. But it wasn't the physical change that impacted Jacob. It was the fact that he finally had to take responsibility for who he was after God made him accept himself. It was then and only then that Jacob experienced true joy.

> Their confused sense of free will and independence has made them prisoners in a life they hate, but joy can set them free if they are willing to make choices based on God's commands.

Joy brings you health. The Bible says, "A merry heart does good, like medicine" (Prov. 17:22). Modern medical science shows that you actually release enzymes that boost your immune system and promotes good health when you laugh. Joy is a great choice to live by.

The world is searching for joy. Choose to be a place where they can find it. Let your home be an *embassy of joy*. When you travel anywhere around the globe, you will find an embassy that represents the United States of America. In that embassy, the laws, customs, and authority of the United States are in full effect. For example, when it is the Fourth of July and Americans at home are celebrating their independence, the United States Embassy in Africa, though halfway around the world, is also celebrating the Fourth of July.

On the third Thursday of November, every United States Embassy will celebrate Thanksgiving, no matter where it is located. Every twenty-fifth of December, a tree will be decorated and Christmas gifts exchanged. No matter how near or how far, there on the grounds of these embassies you will experience life as it is lived and loved in the United States of America.

Likewise, you should be an embassy of the joy of the Lord, no matter what the circumstances are in the world around you. People should find in your life an aura that is not determined by situations or dictated by the world outside but determined by the sovereign presence of God in you. When people see that kind of quality in you, no matter how hostile the world gets, they know they can find a joyful refuge with you.

JOY IS A WEAPON

Joy is a weapon; learn to use it well. Psalm 149:5–6 says:

> Let the saints be joyful...
> Let the high praises of God be in their mouth,
> And a two-edged sword in their hand.

There is a very real conflict in which you and I are engaged every day. It is a fight for our futures. It is a struggle for our successes. It is a battle for our homes, families, and children, and one of the most impacting weapons we can bring with us every day is joy. It reminds the world that no matter how hard it tries, we cannot be defeated. It is a testament that you cannot be conquered and that *quit* is not in your vocabulary. It is your declaration of independence from doubt, discouragement, and despair.

Joy is a choice that will keep you grounded in the midst of the most trying and desperate times. It is truly one of the most unshakable forces on Earth.

Be of good cheer. Do not think of today's failures, but of the success that may come tomorrow. You have set yourselves a difficult task, but you will succeed if you persevere; and you will find a joy in overcoming obstacles. Remember, no effort that we make to attain something beautiful is ever lost.[1]

HELEN KELLER

Legacy—the Only Thing You'll Leave Behind

How Did I Get Here?

I would be remiss if I did not include a quote from Helen Keller in this work. After all, throughout my childhood, her example haunted me every time I told my father that the task before me was impossible. Out of all the sermons that he has ever preached, none are more anointed than those he shared with his children behind closed doors, as he did his utmost to persuade us that we could overcome the world. He would use examples like Helen Keller and a long list of others to illustrate what could be done if you were willing to continue in the effort and not give up.

The frightening reality today is that no matter how much I detested the illustrations when they were shared with me, I find myself introducing my daughter to the story of Miss Keller every time she feels the urge to surrender. You see, the courage to continue was not born in me; it was instilled in me by my father, and he received the same blessed gift from his mother and father, who were instructed in the same fashion by my great-grandparents before them. I guess you could say that it is a part of our legacy.

From one generation to the next, it seems that my family has had a tremendous desire to pass on a heritage of being willing to press forward and give every possible effort to accomplish what God gave each member in the family to do.

It began with the first member of my family to come to the United States one hundred years prior to the signing of the Declaration of Independence. He came from Germany with the Dutch Moravians, and he was filled with the intention to preach the gospel to the New World. His name was John

Hagee. The vessel he traveled the Atlantic on was a ship called *Spirit*. Since his dying breath, there have been forty-eight members of my family who have devoted their lives to full-time gospel ministry. I am number forty-nine.

My great-grandfather John Christopher Hagee, as he lay on his deathbed, asked the Lord to raise up his seed to preach the gospel to the nations of the world. In my lifetime and through my father's ministry, that prayer is being answered. Through the powerful voice of television, the daily broadcast of *John Hagee Ministries* can be seen in 243 nations and territories around the world.

This is not a matter of irony; it is a matter of legacy. The very name of the ministry that is today reaching its arms around the globe is the namesake of those who have come before. Coincidence? Not hardly. Fate? No, it goes well beyond that. It is the plan and purpose of God being fulfilled by consecutive generations of a family that refuses to forget its legacy.

I KNOW WHY I AM HERE

I have never wondered why I was put on this earth. I have felt the purpose of ministry in me all the days of my life. I am the by-product of generations who have answered the call and lived their lives to see the lost won to Christ, and I consider it a high honor to be numbered among them.

It is my prayer that God gives me the wisdom, strength, and courage to run the race that is set before me as valiantly as those before have run theirs. Legacy is a powerful thing. It can push you to limits beyond what others may call reasonable, and it can create in you a sense of urgency and motivation when most are content to be settled and relaxed. Your legacy will outlast any amount of material wealth that you leave behind and will imprint the generations that follow with an identity that will lead them to their destinies.

The time has come for this generation to take account of its legacy and decide what kind of heritage we wish to leave for tomorrow. How do we want the world to remember us? Will we be the generation who held it all together or the one who let it fall apart? Are we willing to answer the hard questions and face the truth, or will we blindly ignore the facts and continue to grope for empty answers instead of finding real solutions? We cannot avoid the difficult issues of our day and believe that if we can camouflage our cowardice long enough, the issues will solve themselves. We must go beyond talking about change to making change.

For us to pretend that our children will be able to handle what we have mismanaged is a farce. It is not reasonable to believe that they will be able to overcome anything without having an example to follow. Without a legacy that will inspire, encourage, and lead them to greater things than we ever achieved, they will fail.

Recently, a study was released describing how each generation had received the benefits of the previous generation to experience a better quality of life than the last. Sadly enough, the end of the study predicted that the next generation of Americans would not have the same quality of life that the current one now enjoys.[2] These findings are proof that no matter how you live your life, you will leave behind a legacy. You cannot escape it, and it will impact those who follow—either for the better or the worse.

Your legacy is both a private and a public matter. You must choose for yourself who you will be, how you will behave, and what kind of legacy you will leave.

No one illustrates this better than Joshua. A quick study of the pages of the Old Testament Book of Joshua will leave you swimming in an ocean of life lessons that will serve all who learn them well. But there are three lessons that I particularly want to extract from the life of Joshua, which will tell you how to leave a legacy that will serve those who follow in your footsteps.

YOU CANNOT IGNORE THE CHALLENGE

All too often, the preferred method of conflict resolution is pretending that the problem doesn't exist. From our earliest accounts of Joshua's life, he shows us the exact way of overcoming a difficult issue. Every time a challenge faced the children of Israel, whom do you find in the middle of it? Joshua!

> Your legacy will outlast any amount
> of material wealth that you leave behind
> and will imprint the generations that
> follow with an identity that will lead
> them to their destinies.

Joshua was out in front of the troops in every battle. When there was a mission that needed to be done, Joshua was the man who volunteered for the adventure. When there were hard questions to be answered, it was Joshua who offered the advice. Why? It was not because he was so brilliant, articulate, and an all-around star but because, more often than not, he was simply willing to be there and unafraid to do the right thing.

Knowing the right thing to do is not nearly as difficult as doing it. You see this in Joshua's announcement to the children of Israel when he and Caleb spied out the land with the other commandos Moses sent across the river. (See Numbers 13.) Ten spies returned to say, "There is no use—we are small; they are huge. If you think we have a chance, you are nuts!" (OK, that's a paraphrase, but you get the point. These guys were discouraged and wanted to ignore the challenge that was before them.)

Not Joshua. The response he and Caleb gave was this: "Let us go up at once and take possession, for we are well able to over-come it" (Num. 13:30).

There was no need to discuss the risks. Joshua and Caleb knew the giants in Canaan were living on land God had set aside for the children of Israel. They asserted, "It's ours; let's go get it." Joshua didn't ignore the reality of giants, but he was not afraid to face them either. The thing that I appreciate about Joshua and his sidekick, Caleb, is that they were not going to exaggerate the problem as their comrades did.

Look at the testimony of the ten spies: "We were like grasshoppers" (v. 33). Come on, I have heard my share of Texas tall tales, but this one takes the cake! A grasshopper is no more than an inch tall. A man is at least sixty inches tall. If those giants made a five-foot man look like a grasshopper, then that would have made the giant more than three hundred feet in height. I do not believe the spies' problems were that big.

We have challenges facing us today that we fail to solve due to the same faulty thinking. Are they big? Indeed! Are they so big we can't overcome them? I don't think so. Look over our nation's past and see some of the huge challenges we, as a people, have overcome. In the short history of this great nation, we have overcome and accomplished more than any other people. We have conquered many of our giants. We have an amazing legacy.

There are a number of challenges facing each of us in the world today. There are enormous economic challenges, political challenges, and spiritual challenges. We can either ignore the giants, or, with God's help, face them believing that the God who has never failed before will not fail us now.

If we neglect the problems of today, we only compound them for tomorrow. We must search within ourselves and be determined that even though there is a struggle to face, we were engineered by God to overcome it. In doing so, we will build a legacy that will inspire our children to have the courage to do the same.

Don't Complain About Today; It Taints Tomorrow

The Bible records that later in the life of Joshua, after he had served his generation and his life was drawing to a close, his generation came to a crossroads. Joshua knew many of the people were making choices that would impact not only them as individuals, but their choices would also impact the nation of Israel as a whole, and they would suffer. He stood before the nation and made this statement: "Choose for yourselves this day whom you will serve, whether the gods which your fathers served that were on the other side of the River, or the gods of the Amorites, in whose land you dwell. But as for me and my house, we will serve the Lord" (Josh. 24:15).

The children of Israel were running through their regular list of complaints. They were comparing themselves to other nations and thinking how much better they would be if they would forfeit their unique, God-given identity and become like everyone else. It's very clear that Joshua let them know they had the freedom to choose as they pleased and suffer the consequences that came with the choice. But as far as Joshua was concerned, "...as for me and my house, we will serve the Lord." Joshua and his family had determined to choose a proper legacy.

This attitude of comparison and complaint seemed to be passed from one generation to the next. A few books later, in

1 Samuel, we read that the children of Israel were at it again. They were looking at all of their neighbors and how they had earthly kings governing them. In spite of the fact that Israel's king was none other than God in heaven, rather than humbly serve Him, they wanted to be like everyone else and have an earthly king they could touch, one comparable to all the other nations of the world.

Where do you think they learned such behavior? The answer is that it was a part of their legacy! It had been passed down to them from one generation to the next, and when it came their time to complain, they weren't going to miss their chance.

For far too long in America, we have mastered the art of complaining. We complain about everything—the way traffic flows in our streets, the service that we receive at restaurants, the leadership of our public officials, the atmosphere at church, the faults of our educational system, and the list could go on and on. Please hear me; there are a lot of things that could use some attention and improvement. But complaining about these things will not get you one step closer to resolution. Don't talk about what you should do; start doing it.

If you need new leadership in your city, find the right person for the job, and elect that person into office. If you need to improve something at the school, don't complain about the system; go join the PTA, and be a part of the solution. If you are looking for things to improve at your church, go knock on your pastor's door and tell him five things that he is doing right. Then let him know that you are here to help and to serve! Believe me; those kinds of conversations go a long way.

When you decide that you can be a part of the answer rather

than just an addition to the endless noise of complaints and rhetoric that fills the air, you've begun to build a legacy of progress and improvement rather than one that teaches your children to find fault in everything around them and pretend their complaints entitle them to a better way of life.

DON'T FORGET WHERE YOU CAME FROM

Both illustrations in the life of Joshua demonstrate that the children of Israel had forgotten where they came from and all that God in heaven did for them. Think of the miracles they saw at the hand of God in such a short period of time.

They were miraculously brought out of Egypt as the result of ten magnificent and horrifying plagues, and they witnessed as God brought the most powerful nation on the earth to its knees.

They saw the Red Sea part for them and then swallow Pharaoh.

They sat in the shade of the cloud by day and were warmed by the fire of His glory at night.

They ate the manna He provided every morning, drank from the water that gushed out of the rock, and saw God's mighty hand defend them in battle.

The list could go on forever. The point is, they forgot what God did for them, and they chose to walk away from His best for their life because they could not see past the current conflict and challenge. This is no way to leave a legacy.

Don't talk about what you should do;
start doing it.

Will you be guilty of the same? Think of all the divine blessings you have seen God pour out on this nation. Look at how He has preserved us and empowered us to be here at this hour in history for such a time as this. Will you ignore every act of divine providence upon this nation and walk away from the opportunity in front of you? Or do you have the courage to at least try to see if God will help you achieve something great?

The choices you make will determine the legacy you leave and the heritage you pass on to your children and your children's children. What will they say about you in time? No one's impact is felt all at once, no matter how great or terrible that person may be. Only history will give the full account of all you were and all you may have failed to be.

Will you be remembered for a valiant and self-sacrificing legacy, or will you be called greedy and irresponsible? Will you turn a deaf ear and a blind eye, ignoring the signs and pretending rather than facing reality?

The choice we make will dictate the label we wear. The danger in doing nothing is that we will lower the standard for our children and create a world where our grandchildren will never know how good life could have been.

We can see this demonstrated in the life of Rehoboam, the son of Solomon and the grandson of David. He had a legacy most monarchs would die for. His father was the wisest and wealthiest man on earth, and his grandfather was a giant-killer and the man after God's own heart. From his pedigree, we should expect great things from Rehoboam. But the contrary is true.

The descriptions of Solomon's royal throne room and the temple he built for God were majestic masterpieces that defy description. They were worth billions in gold, marble, precious stones, and timber. Every item placed in the rooms was a symbol of God's favor upon the house of David and the children of Israel. The king who sat on Solomon's throne in David's city had a heritage that would seem unshakable.

But Rehoboam was a king who chose to play *pretend* rather than face reality. He knew that Israel had problems with idol worship. He knew that idol worship was an issue that removed the favor of God. He knew that the punishment for this behavior was a curse and not a blessing. But out of convenience, he pretended that it really didn't matter.

Rather than address the issue, he ignored it. So God allowed his enemies to enter his father's house and the temple and to carry away all the gold and marble and precious stones. He lost it all in one day. (See 1 Kings 14:21–30.) Among those precious articles were two hundred solid gold shields that the royal guard used to line the path from the throne room in the palace to the temple when King Solomon would go to pray. It was a sight so magnificent that historians said that when Solomon entered the temple, and the Eastern sun reflected from the shields, it seemed as if the arms of God Himself were extended in welcome to the king as he entered the house of the

Lord. Without a doubt, it had to be one of the most impressive displays that the world has ever seen.

Instead of taking any measures to retrieve what was rightfully his, Rehoboam decided on an alternate route that would be easier. He ordered that two hundred shields of brass be made to replace what had been taken. What a tragedy! These shields were used in the same manner as the precious and priceless ones made of gold—but they could not shine as brightly, and they could not compare in value to the shields Solomon hung.

Their lower quality was a reminder to everyone of the precious shields now adorning someone else's wall. Every time that Rehoboam went into the temple, the sun would shine down on the dull, dark bronze metal shields, and people would be reminded that things were no longer as magnificent as they used to be.

This regular reminder of the nation's failure and loss had to be a great source of discouragement. The lowering of the standard lessened the nation's legacy. Pay attention to the real danger in this story as a stark reminder to those of us who read it today. If an Israelite was alive in the days of Solomon's golden shields, that person could remember the glory of the good old days. But all of those born in the nation of Israel *after* the golden shields were taken had no clue what a treasure had been lost. As far as they knew, brass was all there ever was. Their standard was not nearly as high as their fathers' had been, because they had nothing to compare it to. Brass was really all they knew.

This is the point: If our generation allows our standards to slip, our children will never know how good life could truly be. If we allow ourselves to forfeit our freedom on an altar of political correctness, our children will never know the joy of liberty. If we refuse to uphold the standard of truth in our churches, what foundation for the future will those who follow us have? If we enable marriage to be something less than what God ordained in Genesis, what will history record as our legacy? I guarantee that it will not be a gold standard—but something far less.

I recommend that you pay the price of raising the standard, no matter how difficult the task may be. It may not be the easiest route, and it involves sacrifice along the way, but if we have the courage to take it, we will be forever honored for the bold choices we made.

> If our generation allows our standards
> to slip, our children will never know how
> good life could truly be.

It will take great courage to place God back in the mainstream of American life. It will require a level of sacrifice few have ever known. But if we are willing to pay the price today, it will ensure the hope of tomorrow and our legacy.

It is going to take a tremendous amount of faith and fortitude to reestablish the principles of confidence and faith in our generation, but the reward will be a world our children can afford to live in rather than one that threatens their survival.

It will require an extraordinary level of loyalty and integrity to admit all that needs to be sincerely confronted and changed in our world, but if we do not even try, who will? If this is the price of establishing a great legacy, let us be willing to persevere until the price has been paid.

I make this solemn vow to you:

> For the sake of our precious children and our sacred and storied past, I will do my part—even to the final breath I breathe. I will steer my life and the lives of those God gives me to influence down the path of greatness found only in Him so that the remainder of our journey on this earth together can be marked by *success* in spite of struggle and *victory* in the face of the fight. May we each endeavor to lay our lives down so that those who come after us will have the greatest of examples to follow and will find us faithful.

If you are willing to answer the call along with me, then the legacy that we leave will be one that stood its ground in the face of a world that was shaken yet refused to be shattered.

Notes

Chapter 1
Reconnecting With Your Original Design

1.	As quoted in Glenn Van Ekeren, *The Speaker's Sourcebook* (Upper Saddle River, NJ: Prentice Hall, 1994).

Chapter 2
Priorities Will Get You
Where You Want to Go

1.	ThinkExist.com, "William Arthur Ward Quotes," http:// thinkexist.com/quotation/four_steps_to_achievement-plan_ purposefully/329811.html (accessed April 22, 2009).

2.	Jack Canfield and Mark Victor Hansen, *Chicken Soup for the Soul* (Deerfield Beach, FL: Health Communications, 1993), 236–237.

3.	Telford Word, *Unmarried America* (Glendale, CA: Barna Research Group, Ltd., 1993), 22.

Chapter 3
Make a Decision, and Go for It!

1.	ThinkExist.com, "Robert H. Schuller Quotes," http://thinkexist .com/quotation/goals_are_not_only_absolutely_necessary_to/339279 .html (accessed April 23, 2009).

Chapter 4
Pay the Price of Perseverance

1.	QuoteGarden.com, "Quotations About Perseverance," http:// www.quotegarden.com/perseverance.html (accessed April 24, 2009).

2.	Baylor University, "Michael Johnson Profile," http://baylorbears .cstv.com/sports/c-track/mtt/johnson_michael00.html (accessed April 24, 2009).

3.   David Woods, "David Neville Leaves It All on the Track," Indystar.com, August 22, 2008, http://www.indystar.com/apps/pbcs .dll/article?AID=/20080822/SPORTS11/808220480 (accessed March 19, 2009).

Chapter 5
Exude Confidence—the Attitude With Potential

1.   ThinkExist.com, "William Hazlitt Quotes," http://thinkexist .com/quotation/as_is_our_confidence-so_is_our_capacity/227455.html (accessed April 24, 2009).

2.   BrainyQuote.com, "Thomas A. Edison Quotes," http://www .brainyquote.com/quotes/authors/t/thomas_a_edison.html (accessed April 24, 2009).

Chapter 7
Be Identified by Your Integrity

1.   TheQuotationsPage.com, "Classic Quotes," http://www .quotationspage.com/quote/29055.html (accessed April 27, 2009).

2.   The Churchill Centre, "Speeches and Quotes," http://www .winstonchurchill.org/i4a/pages/index.cfm?pageid=388#Poison (accessed April 27, 2009).

Chapter 8
Loyalty—the Quality of Your Character

1.   QuoteDB.com, "Martin Luther King Jr. Quotes," http://www .quotedb.com/quotes/49 (accessed April 27, 2009).

2.   The Stamford Historical Society, "Portrait of a Family: Stamford Through the Legacy of the Davenports," http://www.stamfordhistory.org/ dav_abraham1.htm (accessed May 15, 2009).

Chapter 9
Prayer—the Language of Power

1.   Oswald Chambers, *My Utmost for His Highest*, s.v. August 28.

CHAPTER 10
BE LIBERATED BY YOUR WORSHIP

1.   Kennedy Hickman, "World War I: The Christmas Truce of 1914," About.com: Military History, http://militaryhistory.about.com/od/worldwari/p/xmastruce.htm (accessed April 14, 2009).

CHAPTER 11
JOY—THE CHOICE OF GREATNESS

1.   "Aushwitz Alphabet: Doctors," http://www.spectacle.org/695/doctors.html (accessed April 14, 2009).

2.   "The Numbers Count: Mental Disorders in America," *National Institute of Mental Health*, http://www.nimh.nih.gov/health/publications/the-numbers-count-mental-disorders-in-america/index.shtml (accessed April 15, 2009).

CHAPTER 12
LEGACY—THE ONLY THING YOU'LL LEAVE BEHIND

1.   Helen Keller, in *The Book of Positive Quotations* by John Cook et al., (Minneapolis, MN: Fairview Press, 2007), 642.

2.   Pew Research Center, "Americans See Less Progress on Their Ladder of Life," September 14, 2006, http://pewresearch.org/pubs/319/americans-see-less-progress-on-their-ladder-of-life (accessed April 15, 2009).

PASTOR MATTHEW HAGEE

Matthew Hagee serves as the Executive Pastor of the 20,000 member Cornerstone Church in San Antonio, Texas where he partners with his father, founder Pastor John Hagee to minister to the needs of the church body as well as spread all the Gospel to all the world and to every generation over world wide television.

On October 4, 2003, Matthew married Kendal Elizabeth Young. Together they minister to equip the church of tomorrow how to live the victorious life of the believer. They have been blessed with two children, Hannah Rose Hagee born April 16, 2005, John William Hagee born January 31, 2007 and are expecting their third child this fall.

As their family and ministry grow Matthew and Kendal seek to fulfill the call of God on their lives with the passion and purpose that can only come from the power of family tradition and the anointed call of God on their lives.